Democratic
Principals
in Action

*To educational leaders who
are pioneering school democracy.*

Joseph Blase
Jo Blase
Gary L. Anderson
Sherry Dungan

Democratic Principals in Action

Eight Pioneers

CORWIN PRESS, INC.
A Sage Publications Company
Thousand Oaks, California

For information address:

Corwin Press, Inc.
2455 Teller Road
Thousand Oaks, California 91320

SAGE Publications Ltd.
6 Bonhill Street
London EC2A 4PU
United Kingdom

SAGE Publications India Pvt. Ltd.
M-32 Market
Greater Kailash I
New Delhi 110 048 India

Printed in the United States of America

Library of Congress Cataloging-in-Publication Data

Main entry under title:

Democratic principals in action: Eight pioneers / authors, Joseph
    Blase . . . [et al.].
        p. cm.
    Includes bibliographical references and index.
    ISBN 0-8039-6131-6 (cloth: acid-free paper). — ISBN
0-8039-6132-4 (pbk.: acid-free paper).
        1. School principals—Georgia—Case studies. 2. Educational
leadership—Georgia—Case studies. 3. Teacher participation in
administration—Georgia—Case studies. I. Blase, Joseph.
LB2831.924.G4D45   1995
371.2'012'09758—dc20   94-45029

This book is printed on acid-free paper.

95 96 97 98 99 10 9 8 7 6 5 4 3 2 1

Copy Editor: Tricia Bennett
Production Editor: Yvonne Könneker
Ventura Typesetter: Joe Cribben

72051

Contents

Foreword

This book makes a valuable contribution to our understanding of today's principalship and the challenges of shared governance and democratic leadership. Being more democratic is both challenging and rewarding, and as these eight principals tell their stories, we gain new and important insights into what it means to administer a shared-governance school. Although each of the principals approaches his or her work in a different way, their experiences give us a fresh, new level of understanding about the key ingredients associated with successful democratic leadership.

What do these accounts of leadership tell us? First, the type of leadership and governance undertaken by these principals is not a casual undertaking. Each principal speaks of the special efforts that they have taken to foster leadership among teachers, that is, to empower teachers and encourage their significant involvement in decision making about instruction and other matters related to schools.

When teachers and other stakeholders engage the principal and one another in authentic and open dialogue about what really matters, principals unanimously agree that outcomes improve when *both* teachers and principals collectively share the responsibility to initiate action and to make things better.

Second, it is no coincidence that these principals are strongly oriented toward improving teaching and learning and supporting teachers and, as a result, make things better for children. A key element in their effectiveness is the child-centered and instructionally oriented "end in view" that underlies their leadership perspective. They are motivated to find and support the best practices for children, and they genuinely believe that teachers can and should be trusted to serve those interests. They are committed to opening up a student-centered dialogue with teachers and to trusting that authentic efforts on their part to listen to all teachers will yield better decisions. Although not every principal succeeds to the same degree, there are recurrent themes associated with this orientation toward more democratic leadership: trust in teachers' motives; the ability to listen and to communicate openly; and the willingness to risk letting go of their traditional veto power.

There are a number of recurring challenges associated with these principals' ability to lead democratically. A major frustration encountered is the increased time that is required to involve teachers in decisions, coupled with the difficulty of arranging the daily schedule so that teachers who are participating in shared governance and school leadership activities can be released from classroom responsibilities to work together on governance or instructional improvement projects on a routine basis. Another challenge is that teachers often do not see the need to move beyond their classrooms to take on the schoolwide responsibilities of shared governance. Principals find it important to continuously encourage teachers, to support their interest, and to provide for the regular "care and feeding" of every teacher's interest in shared governance. As teachers gain familiarity and confidence in these activities, their involvement shifts from relatively low-impact to the more high-impact concerns at the crux of school improvement. Two other challenges that the principals face are the need to cultivate central-office support for shared governance and democratic forms of leadership and the continuing need to be deliberate in being open to and hearing all voices within the faculty. Breaking old habits molded by years of working in institutions not designed to encourage democratic forms of leadership or governance requires continuous effort, particularly when many teachers, parents, and administrative colleagues find these familiar ways more comfortable.

The principals studied by Blase et al. are not perfect exemplars of democratic forms of leadership nor is every school a model of shared governance. I am glad that readers are not led to believe that this process is easy or simple; instead, this is a realistic account of these principals' efforts to move toward more democratic forms of school administration. The schools and leaders described here are at various points along a change continuum. For example, whereas some did involve parents and community members in various facets of school governance, most did not. Similarly, whereas some have extended such practices to embrace children and practices within the classroom, most did not. Given the range of democratic governance shown, it is clear that there are different models and that each may be appropriate in a given time and place. The models cannot just be imported to other settings but must organically emerge to fit the unique situation of particular school settings.

Regardless of the particular "end in view," however, it is clear that such forms of school leadership and governance require a strong commitment by administrators to the principle of sharing power with others. It also requires a central administration and a school board that share a commitment to this value. Indeed, several of these principals experienced difficulty because the practices they were attempting to foster at their schools were not well understood, desired, or appreciated by superiors or board members. Similarly, not every school community will have the same readiness for such practices, particularly as these begin to permeate the orientations and experiences of students and change the dynamics and patterns in classrooms. Whether at the school, central-office, board, or community level, principals and teachers who travel this road can expect active as well as passive resistance. Readers who take the challenge that is inherent in striving for more democratic forms of leadership and schooling will find the perspectives of these eight principals useful in anticipating those difficulties and in stimulating strategies for succeeding, in spite of the challenges.

Although school principals have historically been frustrated in their efforts to increase their involvement in the core activities of teaching and learning, the more democratic forms of leadership and shared governance described in this book suggest the possibility of more collegial relations among teachers and school principals. As many of these pioneering principals recount, one of the biggest personal benefits that they have experienced as a result of these new forms of school leadership and shared governance is the greater feeling of satisfaction they gain as a result of working in an authentic collegial partnership with teachers.

Democratic Principals in Action: Eight Pioneers is a must read for principals and teachers committed to shared governance and more democratic forms of leadership.

WILLIAM D. GREENFIELD JR.
PORTLAND STATE UNIVERSITY

Preface

Democratic Principals in Action: Eight Pioneers was written for principals who aspire to democratic leadership. The database for this book was derived from a study of successful principals in schools affiliated with the League of Professional Schools. These principals are true pioneers; although they have only been involved with the league for a few short years, they have made considerable progress in implementing shared-governance (i.e., democratic) structures in their respective situations.

Democratic leadership has received a great deal of attention in the theoretical and practical literature, as well as in the world of practice. However, only a few research-based accounts of this form of leadership have been published. This book focuses on *principals'* perspectives of principals and describes how these principals are facilitating teacher empowerment and the development of democratic structures and processes in a variety of school contexts. The study on which this book is based was designed to illuminate critical aspects of what it means to shared-governance principals to be involved in initiating and implementing teacher empowerment and site-based democracy in schools.

What does democratic leadership look like? How can this approach form strong collegial bonds between educators, enhance teacher empowerment, and lead to schoolwide democratic participation? In another book, *Empowering Teachers: What Successful Principals Do* (Blase & Blase, 1994), Jo Blase and I examined *teachers'* perspectives on effective principal leadership and the effects of such leadership on, for example, teachers' motivation, confidence, commitment, innovation, autonomy, and reflection. In this book, a companion to *Empowering Teachers*, we present portraits that reveal the deeply human challenges confronted by principals who are immersed in learning the lessons of democratic school leadership. These portraits provide valuable lessons about what many consider to be the central challenge of educational administration during the 1990s. *Democratic Principals in Action* moves beyond Blumberg and Greenfield's (1980) well-regarded and high-profile book, *The Effective Principal: Perspectives on School Leadership*, which featured case studies of outstanding traditional principals. In contrast, all the principals discussed here have made substantial progress in empowering teachers and, in several cases, in establishing democratic governance structures in their schools. These principals exemplify that there is a range of approaches to democratic leadership in schools that have embarked on shared-governance or site-based decision making.

Chapter 1 presents a review of selected studies about principal leadership in schools, particularly those published during the 1980s. These studies demonstrate that a "power-over" rather than a "power-with" leadership orientation is most common among principals identified as "effective." The portraits presented in Chapters 2 through 9, however, show principals in the process of developing as democratic leaders; each portrait stands alone and highlights unique characteristics and approaches to leadership. In presenting each principal's perspective on democratic leadership, we avoided evaluating or interpreting what the principals told us. We have not idealized or romanticized their experiences or their perspectives on leadership. You will see principals with varying leadership styles in different situations, struggling through the first few years of implementing shared governance. You will see principals in indeterminate and unpredictable contexts learning and growing, succeeding and failing in their efforts to empower teachers. You will see principals who are challenged by their own inadequacies—men and women who have much to learn yet whose convictions and unrelenting enthusiasm permit them to overcome incredible barriers and to make, in collaboration with teachers, significant advances in implementing new and vital forms of school governance.

Throughout the portraits, we also refrain from offering recipes for success; rather, we present the principals' own words of wisdom and advice as they contemplate the challenges of introducing extensive innovations in typically traditional school settings. It will be up to you, the reader, to interpret the descriptions we present. Each chapter concludes with discussion questions that will encourage you to examine more closely the motivations underlying efforts to establish empowering and democratic schooling.

The book concludes with a summary of our findings about what we call facilitative democratic leadership. In addition, facilitative democratic leadership is discussed in terms of the model of teacher empowerment we have developed.

A word should be said about the geographical context of the study. Like most southern states, Georgia, the site of the study, has changed much in recent decades, but it is also known for its distinctive conservatism, resistance to open and inclusive participation and change, and adherence to bureaucratic tradition. Most of the principals described in this book broke with the past without significant support from central-office personnel, board members, and parents. This, of course, makes their initiatives even more remarkable and noteworthy. Perhaps in such pioneers' successes and challenges we will find the key to initiating our own forms of empowerment.

The authors believe that this book provides valuable descriptive and theoretical information about democratic approaches to school leadership, approaches that are demanded of school reform in the 1990s. We also feel that readers will recognize the courageous persistence of the leaders described herein who are committed to serving the children and adults with whom they work. These leaders have taken on their role of school leadership "with vision-driven, action-oriented, and reflective confidence in their ability to instigate reform and stimulate success" (Roberts, 1990, p. 136). They see their task as a sacred mission and bring to it their deeply held values as well as their passion for redesigning schools to celebrate teaching and learning.

JOSEPH BLASE

Acknowledgments

This book and the research on which it is based would not have been possible without the assistance of many people. We wish to acknowledge the extraordinary school leaders who generously consented to be a part of our inquiry; their pioneering work with the League of Professional Schools stands as a shining example of wonderful possibilities for today's schools. We also wish to acknowledge Dr. Lew Allen, an associate of the League of Professional Schools, who served as an adviser to our research and writing efforts. As always, we deeply appreciate the hard work of our clerical staff—Donna Bell, Linda Edwards, and Frances White—and our editor, Cheryl Smith. We also benefited greatly from the thoughtful feedback of several superb practitioners, including David Curry, Pam Johns, Betty Keene, and Annette Nichols. Finally, funding in the form of a grant from the Spencer Foundation enabled us to undertake a project that would have otherwise been impossible; the interest and support of the people at the Spencer Foundation was consistently encouraging and rewarding.

JOSEPH BLASE
JO BLASE
GARY L. ANDERSON
SHERRY DUNGAN

About the Authors

Joseph Blase is Professor of Educational Leadership at the University of Georgia. Since receiving his Ph.D. in 1980 from Syracuse University, his research has focused entirely on understanding the work lives of teachers. He has published many studies in the areas of teacher stress, relations between teachers' personal and professional lives, teacher socialization, and principal-teacher relationships. His recent work, which focuses on school-level micropolitics, received the 1988 Davis Memorial Award given by the University Council for Educational Administration. He edited *The Politics of Life in Schools: Power, Conflict, and Cooperation* (Sage, 1991); coauthored, with Peggy Kirby, *Bringing Out the Best in Teachers: What Effective Principals Do* (Corwin Press, 1992); and coauthored, with Jo Blase, *Empowering Teachers: What Successful Principals Do* (Corwin Press, 1994). He is currently coauthoring a book about the micropolitics of school leadership.

Jo Blase is Associate Professor of Educational Leadership at the University of Georgia and a former public school teacher, principal, and director of staff development. She received her Ph.D. in educational administration, curriculum, and supervision in 1983 from the University of Colorado at Boulder. Through work with the Beginning Principal Study National Research Team, the League of Professional Schools, and educators with whom she consults, she has pursued her interest in preparation for and entry to educational and instructional leadership as it relates to supervisory discourse. Winner of the 1983 American Association of School Administrators Outstanding Research Award, her recent publications include articles in the *Journal of Staff Development*, the *Journal of Curriculum and Supervision*, and the *Alberta Journal of Educational Research* and a co-authored book, with Joseph Blase, *Empowering Teachers: What Successful Principals Do* (Corwin Press, 1994). She has also authored chapters on becoming a principal, school renewal, supervision, and organizational discourse. Currently, she is conducting research on supervisory discourse among physicians as medical educators.

Gary L. Anderson is Associate Professor of Educational Administration at the University of New Mexico. He received his Ph.D. in curriculum and instruction from Ohio State University in 1988 and has since focused his research on democratic leadership, critical ethnography, Latin American education, and the relationship of critical theory and sociology to educational leadership. His recent publications include articles in *Educational Administration Quarterly* and *Review of Educational Research*; a coedited book, with Martha Montero-Sieburth, *Latin American Ethnographic Research*; and a co-authored book, with Kathryn Herr and Ann Nihlen, *Studying Your Own School: An Educator's Guide to Qualitative Practitioner Research* (Corwin Press, 1994).

Sherry Dungan is Assistant Professor at the University of Alabama in the area of professional studies and a former public school teacher and reading specialist. She received her Ed.D. in educational leadership as a 1993 Graduate of Distinction from the University of Georgia. While on the faculty of Appalachian State University in Boone, North Carolina, she received the 1993 Association for Supervision and Curriculum Development Dissertation of the Year Award for her research in the area of instructional supervision and was a Division A finalist for the 1993 American Educational Research Association's Dissertation of the Year Award. A recent publication appears in *School Organization,* and her work includes various monographs and pieces in regional journals. Her research continues to focus on the communicative and cultural aspects of supervisory conferencing, leadership, and teacher empowerment.

To move a school toward a community of leaders [implies] a level of personal security on the part of both principal and teacher. To publicly articulate a personal vision, relinquish control, empower and entrust teachers, involve teachers early, accord responsibility to untried and aspiring teacher-leaders, share responsibility for teacher failure, accord responsibility to teachers for success, and have confidence that all teachers can lead, a principal has to be a secure person willing to take risks.

—Roland S. Barth (1988, p. 142)

1

Studying Principals' Leadership

This book is based on a study of eight shared-governance (i.e., democratic) principals whose respective schools are members of the League of Professional Schools in Georgia, directed by Carl Glickman (1993). The league's purpose is to establish representative, democratic decision-making structures to promote teacher involvement in schoolwide instructional and curricular decisions. Action research, a central component of shared governance, involves school staff members in collecting, analyzing, and interpreting data to assess the effects of shared decision making on students, teachers, administrators, and parents and to improve decision-making processes and outcomes; made through elected, representative governing bodies, these decisions often relate to areas such as staff development, educational materials and innovations, classroom management, and budgeting for instruction. The league does not prescribe specifically how member schools are to realize their commitment to shared governance. Instead, educators in each school are encouraged to create policies and procedures consistent with the school's unique situation. At the time of this study, each of these eight principals and their schools had been affiliated with the league for 3 years, since its inception in the fall of 1990. (See Resource A for more about the league.)

The eight principals described in this book were considered pioneers by their school faculties and the league staff. Each principal participated in a series of intensive interviews that explored central aspects of their perspectives on democratic leadership. Some of the topics that were explored included principals' development as democratic leaders, their purposes and goals, the strategies they used to implement shared governance, major problems and crises, and sources of stress/failure and success/satisfaction. (See Resource A for a full description of the research problem and procedures.)

In recent years, interest in school restructuring and, in particular, democratic-empowering forms of school leadership has increased significantly. Discussions of differences between power-over and power-with approaches to leadership have helped to clarify conceptual differences between these two approaches and to explain the implications of each for the practice of school leadership. Power-over leadership approaches emphasize control and manipulation of others' behavior, thoughts, and values. In contrast, power-with approaches to leadership focus on the development of collegiality, reciprocity, equality, and mutuality with others (Dunlap & Goldman, 1991; Kreisberg, 1992). The study of eight shared-governance principals on which this book is based actually reveals incidents of both types of leadership; it portrays the mix of power-over and power-with leadership that occurs in real life. This book describes several principals who, against many odds, actually enact quite efficacious power-with approaches to leadership.

Most research on school principals has taken place in traditional schools. Consequently, the leadership style of principals identified as effective is generally consistent with hierarchical, top-down organizational structures. Effective school leaders typically are described as strong, decisive, directive, take charge visionaries who tend to be predominantly control oriented in their relationships with teachers. We hope to demonstrate that such a perspective on leadership is, in many respects, inconsistent with school-restructuring programs that attempt to dismantle bureaucratic structures and implement democratic structures and processes to empower teachers and others. To begin, we review the many prominent studies and perspectives on effective school principals available in the professional literature over the last 3 decades.

Studies of School Principals

According to Bridges (1982), studies of school principals conducted during the 1960s and 1970s fall into three categories: (a) antecedents of principal behavior, (b) the content of principal behavior, and (c) the outcomes of principal behavior. Antecedents refer to person-related and role-related variables and include studies of attitudes (such as satisfaction) and traits (such as age and experience). Expectations and power (especially sources of power, à la French & Raven, 1959) were research topics emphasized by the role-related approach. Unidimensional studies of principal behavior centered on single behaviors such as risk taking, mobility, and evaluation; multidimensional studies of behavior were usually conducted with the Leadership Behavior Description Questionnaire. A second approach to the study of behavior—the activity approach (see Mintzberg, 1973)—examined the actual content and character of principals' work (which includes activities that principals carry out). Finally, research on outcomes focused on the effects of principals' actions on, for example, teacher morale and school climate. Studies of principal effectiveness also appeared frequently in this segment of the literature; however, by comparison, studies of principal effects on student achievement have been rare (Bridges, 1982).

Greenfield (1982), in his review of the literature, concluded that the early seminal work on school principals by Foskett (1967); Gross and Herriott (1965); Hemphill, Griffiths, and Frederiksen (1962); and Lipham and Franks (1966) laid the foundation for the type of research produced during the 1980s. However, with the exception of a few studies (e.g., McPherson, Salley, & Baehr, 1975; Wolcott, 1973), what principals actually do within the sociopolitical, cultural, and organizational milieu in which they work has seldom been explored.

Wolcott's (1973) ground-breaking ethnographic study was the first to provide thick descriptions of the actions and purposes of a single elementary school principal. Wolcott found that the principal he studied spent most of his time in "an almost endless series of encounters" (p. 88) that consisted of receiving requests and responding to problems, orienting and greeting people, and monitoring the school building. Wolcott's research provided early evidence of findings echoed by later research (see Crowson & Porter-Gehrie, 1980; Martin & Willower, 1981; Peterson, 1978). He concluded that although principals were often expected to be agents of change, the reality was that they are "monitors of continuity of institutions and society" (p. 321). Wolcott also noted that principals were consumed by administrative responsibilities as well as interpersonal conflicts, and, as a result, they tended to devote limited attention to instructional leadership.

In a widely publicized nationwide survey study of over 700 principals, McPherson et al. (1975) described the basic functions of the principal's job in relation to the varying conditions of the work setting. These researchers found that school type and school size accounted for most of the variance in what principals actually do on the job. Socioeconomic status, ethnic composition, and teaching staff also contributed to this variance but less significantly. McPherson et al. were among the first to demonstrate that leadership style varied with school context. They wrote, "It seems axiomatic that principals who perform successfully in these different types of principalship will have different interests, skills and leadership styles" (p. 7). Like Wolcott (1973), these authors concluded that few principals enacted a form of leadership that emphasized instruction, change, and improvement:

> Our data analysis suggests that, to a certain extent, principals are captives of their environments. This is not to intimate that some individual principals will not overcome organizational obstacles in performing their work and changing their particular school environment. What we do suggest is that the commonly expressed idea that principals are or should be change agents may be subject to considerable revision. (p. 8)

Metz's (1978) case studies of life in two junior high schools produced vivid descriptions of what principals with contrasting leadership styles do in governing their schools. Metz depicted one of the principals she studied as authoritarian, bureaucratic, and parental. She states, however, that this principal saw himself as persuasive and suggestive. This study provides an early example of how one principal manipulated and controlled teachers, apparently without their knowledge, through subtle and indirect means. Metz writes:

> The discrepancy between Mr. Brandt's rhetoric and his practice . . . annoyed his teachers. But it did not lead to rebellion. He succeeded in controlling them and to getting their compliance without much objection primarily by controlling their definition of the character of the school. He created an impression that the way he asked them to conduct themselves and to direct the children at Chauncey was inherent in the inevitable character of public schools. It was not a matter of his personal decision but simply given in the nature of things. Teachers accepted this definition of things. (p. 192)

In addition, her research highlighted a problem that others have examined more recently regarding the discrepancy between how principals see themselves and how they are viewed by others, especially teachers (Argyris, 1982; Johnston & Venable, 1986).

Studies of Effective Principals

During the 1980s, significant research attention was given to the study of effective school principals. Whereas research in the 1960s and 1970s relied heavily on surveys and statistical methods, greater use of qualitative methods—in-depth case studies, ethnographies, and longitudinal observation—was made during the 1980s (Hall, 1992). This development paralleled the effective schools research (e.g., Edmonds, 1979) and called for greater accountability and strong leadership in American public education. Although only a small number of qualitative studies of effective principals actually were published during the 1980s, these studies provide descriptions of the types of strong and effective leadership that were touted during the 1980s and preceding decades and, by and large, continue to dominate conceptions of effectiveness in the 1990s.

Examination of this line of inquiry demonstrates that effective school principals were predominantly controlling in their relationships with teachers. However, such control was frequently enacted through diplomatic and sometimes subtle means and was compatible with the normative structure of the situations in which principals worked. Descriptions of facilitative-democratic approaches to leadership rarely appeared in the professional literature generated during the 1980s, although effective principals were often described, in comparison with principals in general, as open, collaborative, and quasi-participatory.

Blumberg and Greenfield's (1980) high-profile interview-based study of eight effective principals underscored that there are a variety of approaches to effective school leadership and that these vary from one setting to another. The authors describe one principal whose leadership was based on problem solving, another whose political skills promoted success, and a third whose humanism was central to his effectiveness. All the principals that were studied emphasized the importance of building mutually supportive administrative-faculty relations and the ability to "listen" to teachers.

Blumberg and Greenfield's study also suggested that although effective principals' influence on teachers was frequently based on exchange processes, such processes were consistent with school- and systemwide norms and goals. Exchange theories assume that individuals (and groups) attempt to maximize their gains (rewards, benefits, profits) and minimize the costs of social interaction to secure valued outcomes (Homans, 1958). What is exchanged can be material or nonmaterial (Homans, 1958), economic or psychological (Foa & Foa, 1974). The comments of one of the principals interviewed by Blumberg and Greenfield (1980) illustrate this approach to influencing teachers:

> They made it obvious to me what they expected. They wanted more strict enforcement of student discipline codes. . . . They wanted administrators around the building; they wanted you to be visible. . . . As you fulfill their expectations, also

taking into consideration your own priorities, you build one hell of an alliance with your faculty. You really get them in your corner, so when the time comes for you to ask them to do something they would not normally do, they'll do it. (p. 111)

Blumberg and Greenfield (1980) concluded that although the eight principals they studied held idiosyncratic perspectives toward their work, three major factors accounted for their success: (a) They all wanted to make schools over in their image (vision), (b) they assumed a very proactive leadership orientation, and (c) they were resourceful in structuring their jobs and time to pursue personal objectives as principals. Implicitly, principal effectiveness was defined in terms of a power-over (i.e., control-oriented) approach to leadership rather than a power-with (i.e., collegial, democratic) approach (Kreisberg, 1992). However, their approach was not considered offensive or obtrusive because they seldom used harsh authoritarian or overtly controlling practices.

Lightfoot's *The Good High School* (1983) presented detailed portraits of six schools located in different regions of the United States. The principals of these schools are described as critical actors in each portrait. Consistent with Blumberg and Greenfield (1980), Lightfoot found that each effective principal exhibited a different leadership style (e.g., traditional authoritarian, paternalistic, quasi-participatory), each style made sense in the particular situation, and all six principals were considered change agents. Of particular importance is the conclusion that successful leadership was not defined solely in terms of strong masculine traits but included traditionally female characteristics such as nurturance, receptivity, and responsiveness to relationships and context. Lightfoot (1983) also found some evidence of collective decision making in the high schools studied. Such factors notwithstanding, principals' interactions with teachers were, in part, described in terms of the same type of exchange and control dynamics noted by Blumberg and Greenfield (1980).

The following quote about a principal named Mastruzzi reveals the relationship between exchange and control:

The principal's bountiful patience and generosity are not mere gifts, they are part of an exchange; he expects something in return. Says one admirer, "He gives with a full heart, but he expects a fair exchange . . . " "He never says no to us, and he expects we will never say no to him." (Lightfoot, 1983, p. 340)

Lightfoot (1983) continues, "For Mastruzzi less imperial control and more dispersion of power buys him increased faculty commitment and loyalty" (p. 340). Once again, the importance of subtle and indirect methods of control is apparent.

The Cultural Perspective

The inability of traditional scientific inquiry to produce practical knowledge and inform practice in school leadership (Sergiovanni & Corbally, 1984) and new theoretical understandings of schools as loosely coupled organizations (Weick, 1976) challenged the efficacy of rational-bureaucratic models of school organization and hierarchical forms of leadership. During the 1980s and 1990s the cultural perspective on schools has been advanced by educational scholars as a new and more effective means with which to control teachers, especially in the area of instruction. Practitioners have been advised to manage the school's values, rituals, and shared meanings in addition to bureaucratic mechanisms (e.g., rules, policies) to gain teacher compliance.

Sergiovanni and Corbally's (1984) comments illustrate the value/ moral dimensions of organizational life that are revealed through the cultural perspective. Referring to the principals studied by Wolcott (1973) and Metz (1978), they write:

These principals were less managers of an enterprise in pursuit of stated objectives and more priests charged with the responsibility of maintaining and extending the existing social order and set of accompanying moral precepts. The schools in question were more sacred organizations, protective of a set of values and dedicated to socializing others to these values, than instrumental organizations, designed to effectively and efficiently pursue certain academic objectives. (p. 119)

Some educational scholars have described approaches that principals can use for the management of school culture. Firestone and Wilson (1985) discuss how school principals can manipulate "cultural linkages" through symbolic activities (e.g., rituals, celebrations, recognitions, slogans) that directly influence teachers' consciousness and "affect the way . . . [they] (and students) think about their work" (p. 8). The authors argue that because teachers are often isolated from one another and because of their vulnerability to intrusions on their authority, they may

> view . . . the principal as a powerful, wise individual whose praise is meaningful and protection is sure. . . . As a result, teachers invest a good deal of affect in their view of the principal; the office is a symbolic one that can be used to manipulate the stories and rituals that interpret teachers' work. (p. 21)

In spite of the incredible amount of interest in the notion of school culture in the field of educational administration over the last 10 years, few published studies have focused directly on how principals manage culture to influence teachers. In our view, even cultural studies of democratic, empowering, and collegial forms of principal leadership provide no evidence that teachers, in general, receive substantial opportunities to engage in open dialogue and to participate fully in democratic decision making at the school level.

For example, Leithwood and Jantzi (1990) examined the practices of 12 effective principals in schools with collaborative cultures. As transformational leaders, these principals used bureaucratic and cultural mechanisms, including staff development; communication about cultural norms, values, and beliefs; and power sharing to enhance teachers' individual and collective problem-solving capacities.

Although the actions of the 12 principals that were studied enhanced collaboration between teachers and principals, we would argue that the data also suggest that principals frequently used cultural linkages to control teachers in predetermined directions. The teachers who took part in this study seemed to have some input in decision making, and principal-teacher relationships were defined as collaborative. However, Leithwood and Jantzi (1990) provide no evidence that teachers were treated as equal partners in making a broad range of educational and organizational decisions. Indeed, the type of transformational leadership described by Leithwood and Jantzi appears to be a contemporary form of strong leadership, one that emphasizes cultural rather than bureaucratic forms of influence and control.

In fact, what these authors have called transformational leadership may be the kind of transformational leadership frequently touted in the management literature. It is fundamentally control oriented and based on exchange processes and use of normative influence strategies and goals. Bennis and Nanus's (1985) description of Lee Iacocca's leadership at Chrysler is a good example of this strong leadership perspective.

> He provided the leadership to transform a company from bankruptcy to success. He created a vision of success and mobilized large factions of key employees to align behind the visions. . . . He empowered them [Chrysler employees]. (p. 17)

Bennis and Nanus's description of Iaccoca is a gross oversimplification of transformational leadership; dynamic, open, and democratic interaction between leaders and others is noticeably absent, and the decisional authority and responsibility of others are limited significantly.

Reitzug and Reeves (1992) describe how one elementary school principal used symbolic leadership to influence school culture. The authors point out that although the principal did not push his ideas concerning a particular curricular approach, many of his actions effectively communicated his preferences to teachers. Through modeling, placing articles in teachers' mailboxes, doing classroom walk-throughs, and making suggestions, the principal successfully shaped school culture according to his vision. At the same time, the authors interpret the principal's behavior as more empowering than manipulative. Teachers were not forced to do things in a particular way; instead, the principal insisted that teachers examine and critique their own situations to improve them.

Two points should be made with regard to Reitzug and Reeves's (1992) conclusions. First, given teachers' sensitivity and responsiveness to the expectations of principals in general, however diplomatically these expectations are expressed, teachers cannot be expected to feel totally free to use their own judgment in making decisions. In fact, in a recently published study of 11 shared-governance principals, Blase and Blase (1994) found that teachers frequently attempted to "please the principal." Other studies consistently have shown that teachers tend to be politically conservative and submissive in their relationships with school principals (Goodlad, 1983; Lortie, 1975).

Second, although the principal's actions enhanced teachers' capacity for critique in relation to instruction, this did not result in increased democratic participation by teachers. Reitzug and Reeves (1992) provide no evidence of teacher participation in formal school-wide democratic structures and processes nor is there evidence to indicate that teachers addressed democratic issues related to social justice and equality (Foster, 1986; Giroux, 1992).

Parkay and Hall (1992) and associates on the research team of the Beginning Principal Study examined the leadership of 12 effective beginning principals. One of these principals was identified as an exemplary 1990s principal and subsequently described by Hall (1992) as a believer in strong administrative leadership as advocated by the effective schools research of the 1980s (e.g., Edmonds, 1979). Descriptions of this beginning principal are remarkably consistent with how the previously reviewed studies have described effective principals. Hall's principal set expectations for the school, encouraged two-way communication with the faculty, used data to make decisions, and was highly visible and caring. For this principal, empowerment meant listening to the teachers and enhancing the authority of his administrators. To be more explicit, Hall is illustrating a strong, control-oriented approach to the principalship. The principal's expectations shaped much of what occurred in the school. Even his attempts to empower others are narrowly circumscribed by his own goals.

In another study of cultural leadership, Anderson (1991) directly examined the complex process of ideological control and cognitive politics that is practiced by principals in one suburban school district. He described how school principals overtly and subtly attempted to control teachers by managing language. Anderson found that promotion of a conflict-free vocabulary in the schools was the medium through which principals worked to create a culture of harmony and consensus. By discussing several problems in the school district, Anderson illustrates how principals intervene and attempt to use language to define reality for teachers.

Ball (1987) has generated detailed descriptions of the major leadership styles—managerial, interpersonal, and authoritarian—of school heads (i.e., principals) from case studies of British schools. Ball argued that although each leadership style was identified with the use of different strategies/practices and that each had different effects on teachers, all were fundamentally designed to control teachers. For example, interpersonally oriented principals attempted to control teachers through the use of private persuasion, high visibility, consideration, and exchange, as well as illusion, role prescription, and the manipulation of resources. Ball concluded that teacher participation in all the schools studied was at best pseudoparticipation: Teacher input was consultative; open exchange and democratic interaction between school heads and teachers seldom occurred.

Blase (1993) studied the perspectives of over 800 teachers on the power/influence orientations of open and effective school principals. In his study, major strategies identified with effective principals were consistent with those identified in other research. These included rewards, communication of expectations, support, formal authority, modeling, visibility, and suggestion. An empowerment strategy was also identified with effective principal leadership, but this strategy was used very infrequently compared with those identified above. Blase defines the term *normative instrumental leadership* as an orientation in which control of teachers is central, and such control is enacted primarily through a process of exchange. His study suggests that our best school principals largely attempt to control both the ends and means of teachers' work in schools. In contrast to closed and ineffective principals, they use strategies and pursue goals that are generally acceptable to teachers. Blase concluded:

> Effective school principals typically fail to include teachers
> in decision making or limit their involvement significantly.

Teachers rarely identify their fundamental needs, values, and aspirations. . . . Compliance is a typical response of teachers to . . . open/effective principals. . . . Effective principals articulate their visions, set their goals, explain their expectations, and, in large part, determine the means to achieve such ends. Simply stated, teachers are normatively influenced "to buy into the principals' agenda." (p. 158)

The Control Perspective

A number of factors probably account for the dominance of the control orientation observed in studies of school principals. Some principals undoubtedly have strong needs to dominate others (Kipnis, 1976; Winter, 1973). Moreover, the bureaucratic nature of schools emphasizes rational-legal authority associated with position, policies, rules, regulations, and procedures. Such control mechanisms were expanded by the legislative mandates produced during the 1980s (Chubb & Moe, 1986). A rational-control orientation toward schooling has also been fostered by the school-effectiveness literature and related approaches to school improvement.

Bates (1986) contends that the control orientation also appears to be prominent among many scholars in educational administration. This may be a function of strong identification with an epistemology that adheres to a scientific view of administration on the basis of the ability to produce lawlike generalizations and to predict accurately (Smith & Blase, 1991). That practicing administrators should work to expand their control over teachers seems to be a tacit assumption among such scholars. Hoy and Brown (1988), for example, write:

A major task of leaders is to get individuals to comply with their directives. Formal authority is satisfactory for eliciting certain minimum performance levels, but it is not sufficient for obtaining compliance beyond formal and bureaucratic expectations. Therefore, a basic challenge before principals is to extend their influence over their professional staff beyond the narrow limits of formal authority. (pp. 33-34)

During the last decade, many scholars of educational administration have recognized the limitations of using direct forms of control, primarily because of potential resistance from teachers. However, control has not been rejected as the dominant orientation. On the contrary, increasing control through more subtle cultural and ideological means has been advocated as an effective leadership strategy (Deal & Kennedy, 1984; Firestone & Wilson, 1985). There is even some evidence that such forms of control are increasing in prominence in educational settings (Anderson, 1991; Sparks, 1988). New approaches to school organization (such as site-based management, shared governance, and participatory leadership), however, emphasize the importance of authentic forms of democratic-transformational leadership as well (Schlechty, 1990).

Moreover, research on site-based governance in schools underscores the problem of principal control. Malen and Ogawa's (1988) districtwide case study of site-based governance councils in Salt Lake City, Utah, is one of the most dramatic examples of how principals effectively undermined site-based council governance structures. Although these councils were given broad authority in formal policy making, parity protection (e.g., equal voting protection), and training provision, teachers and parents actually had little influence. In many cases, principal control was exercised informally and subtly. Teachers who participated in the Malen and Ogawa study indicated that principal control was related to teachers' fear of sanctions; for example, being labeled a troublemaker was described as one form of sanction. In addition, their data suggest that principal control has resulted in the development of a subordinate orientation in teachers. The comments of two teachers are illustrative: "You learn to take the principal's lead," and "If the principal lets [his or her] opinions be known, you learn to follow suit" (p. 257). This implies that the successful implementation of democratic structures in schools will require substantial resocialization of both school principals and teachers.

Directly and indirectly, studies of principals indicate that control is the dominant leadership style of even open and effective principals. Furthermore, although research has generated some data about principals' use of participatory approaches to teachers, these are studies of principals who work in traditional schools and who, for the most part, use traditional approaches to leadership (Ball, 1987; Blase, 1993). The extant studies of principals underscore the salience of a power-over approach to teachers that is characterized by the use of power/influence to control teachers' behavior, thoughts, or values (Blase, 1993; Dunlap & Goldman, 1991; Kreisberg, 1992). As suggested, such an approach to teachers was advanced by the effective schools research (Edmonds, 1979; Purkey & Smith, 1983), as well as other first-wave educational reform efforts especially prominent in the United States during the 1980s, and reflects the pattern of control orientations that has characterized educational systems in the United States.

Facilitative-Democratic Leadership

Reports by the Carnegie Commission on Teaching as a Profession (1986), the Holmes Group Executive Board (1986), and the Education Commission of the States (Green, 1986) precipitated a second wave of educational reform. In contrast to earlier efforts, second-wave reformists have advocated fundamental changes in the governance structures of schools to enhance teacher professionalism, teacher autonomy, and teacher empowerment. They have argued that teachers' knowledge/expertise, especially in the areas of curriculum, teaching, and learning, should play a major role in decision making at the school level (Barth, 1990; Bolin, 1989; Conley & Bacharach, 1990; Maeroff, 1988).

At the same time, reformists have recognized the critical role of principal support and facilitative-democratic leadership in initiating, implementing, and sustaining viable forms of shared decision making at the school level (Aronstein, Marlow, & Desilets, 1990; Chapman, 1988; Duke, Showers, & Imber, 1980; Malen & Ogawa, 1988). An orientation of this nature can be referred to as a power-through (Dunlap & Goldman, 1991) or a power-with approach to leadership. In both cases, administrators facilitate the development of collegial and reciprocal norms. Dialogue with teachers based on sharing, mutuality, and equality is encouraged; however, this occurs to a significantly lesser extent in a power-through versus a power-with approach.

Thus far, a few empirical studies of facilitative-democratic leadership have been produced. Although some studies have examined a variety of factors associated with such leadership, most have focused on characteristics of principals or its effects on teacher empowerment. Studies of leadership characteristics reveal the centrality of factors such as principal trust (Clift, Johnson, Holland, & Veal, 1992; Lindle, 1991; Martin, 1990), respect for teachers (Clift et al., 1992; Etheridge & Hall, 1991; Lindle, 1991), support for staff development (Kasten, Short, & Jarmin, 1989), praise (Kasten et al., 1989), vision (Kasten et al., 1989), support of teachers' decisions (Clift et al., 1992), listening (Clift et al., 1992), and providing adequate time (Kasten et al., 1989) for the development of cooperative relationships with teachers.

Studies of facilitative-democratic leadership and its effects on teacher empowerment include Bredeson's (1989) study that lists several factors that enhance teacher empowerment, including listening, providing supportive resources, being visible, having trust, giving praise and feedback, following through on teacher decisions, and being involved. Reitzug (1994) conceptualizes and describes three categories of principal behavior—support, facilitation, and possibility—that contribute to teacher empowerment. Melenyzer (1990) produced a lengthy list of principal leadership factors (e.g., vision, recognition, visibility, decisiveness, respect, support for shared decision making, and support for collegiality) that positively affect teacher empowerment.

Kirby and Colbert (1992) found that principal authenticity (an increased degree of genuineness) was related to teachers' perceptions of empowerment. Blase and Blase (1994) have produced detailed descriptions of seven major strategies: (a) demonstrating trust in teachers, (b) developing shared-governance structures, (c) encouraging teacher input, (d) encouraging teacher autonomy, (e) encouraging teacher innovation, (f) giving rewards, and (g) providing support. An additional category of personal characteristics (i.e., caring, enthusiasm, optimism, honesty, friendliness) completes Blase and Blase's descriptions that comprise effective facilitative-democratic leadership.

Case Studies of
Shared-Governance Principals

Clearly, the number of empirical studies of democratic leadership is limited. This book presents robust descriptions and new understandings of democratic leadership from the perspectives of principals who work in a variety of school contexts and who have developed unique approaches to initiating and implementing various forms of shared governance in their schools. The eight principals that we describe are not perfect; contradictions, shortcomings, and confusions are apparent among them all. They are real leaders who are immersed in the beginning stages of shared governance. As such, they are struggling constantly with internal and external barriers to implementing viable forms of teacher empowerment and democratic structures and processes. As readers will see, the changes that accompany the drive toward participation, democracy, and equity can be uncomfortable and messy but infinitely rewarding as well. Ultimately, of course, the reader should explore the cases we present and construct for him- or herself a perspective on democratic leadership appropriate to his or her situation.

In Chapters 2 through 9 we describe the unique perspectives of eight exceptional shared-governance principals. The four perspectives described in Chapters 2 through 5 illustrate a teacher professionalism-participation orientation. Principals with this orientation focused on the development of teachers as professionals; less attention was given to fully using democratic structures and processes to generate democratic outcomes. These principals encouraged teacher input in decision making, supported the development of teachers' technical knowledge and skill, and promoted risk-free environments to increase creativity and innovation in the classroom. However, they also limited the development of teachers' participation in schoolwide decision making by using vetoes, identifying nonnegotiables, making unilateral decisions, controlling hiring, and monitoring. At the same time, in contrast to all of the other principals we studied, two of the empowerment-oriented principals actively pursued student equity issues.

The perspectives of the four principals described in Chapters 6 through 9 demonstrate a concern with democratic structures and processes as well as teacher empowerment. In contrast to the teacher professionalism-participation principals, these administrators showed a deeper and more complex understanding of individual and organizational power. They also encouraged increased involvement by teachers in democratic structures and processes, not only to achieve school improvement goals but also to experience and come to understand the process. Operationally, these principals supported teachers' role as decision makers; teachers were encouraged to accept decisional authority in both instructional and noninstructional high-impact areas of school life. In addition, viable decisional structures (e.g., committees) and processes were set up to promote complete teacher participation. To create equal collegial relationships with teachers, principals with this perspective seldom used vetoes, made unilateral decisions, or defined nonnegotiable areas of decision making. It should be mentioned that at this writing all of the principals we studied emphasized empowering and/or democratic relationships with teachers. However, the inclusion of other stakeholders, such as parents and students, had not yet been addressed.

In Chapter 10 we summarize and discuss findings presented in the previous chapters of the book. Differences between the professional, participatory, and empowerment leadership orientations derived from our data are discussed further. The book concludes with a brief note about obstacles to implementing shared democracy and empowerment.

2

A Democratic Leader

Eliciting Teacher Voice and Monitoring Student Equity

There's going to be some criticism. There are going to be people who like you, and there are going to be people who don't like you. You're going to be misunderstood. And all of those things, of course, exist whether you are authoritarian or whether you're democratic. But when you're democratic you're going to hear about it, and when you're authoritarian you're not going to hear about it. And I'd rather hear about it.

—Linda Jackson, Principal
Harriett Wilson Elementary School

Not only did Linda Jackson not set out to be a principal, but she did not even set out to be a teacher. Although both of her parents were teachers, she decided to study computers and worked for many years as a computer programmer. When her family moved from Washington, D.C., to California, she began volunteering at her children's school and discovered that she loved working with children. That experience prompted her to go back to school to get her teacher certification, which led to a 15-year career as a teacher. Now Linda is in her fourth year as principal of Harriett Wilson Elementary School, located in a working-class suburban neighborhood in the South. All of the students at Harriett Wilson are African American, and 60% of the teaching staff is African American and 40% is white.

Eliciting Teacher Voice

As a teacher, Linda had the good fortune to work under principals who exhibited open and democratic leadership styles. She also had experience working on leadership teams, first in California and then in Illinois:

> We had a leadership team in California, and it made a lot of decisions. It provided for not just dissemination of information but also a way to voice concerns from the grade levels up. I was on the leadership team 3 out of the 5 years I was there, and I liked working with a group. I moved to Illinois and had an opportunity again to be part of a leadership team.

Furthermore, she was used to seeing teachers and parents on interview committees when she interviewed for teaching positions. It was not until she moved back to the southern state in which she grew up that she encountered authoritarian administrators.

> As far as I was concerned, there was no teacher involvement here in any decisions that were made. There was a structure for shared decision making, but the district said you will have a leadership team, so every school had one. This district said we would have a leadership team and that it would be composed of grade-level chairpersons. The principal asked me to be on the leadership team. And for a long time, we wondered what our role was, what were we supposed to do? We had release time every week, but we didn't know what we were supposed to talk about. For a while we didn't even meet with the principal, who was very, very authoritarian. That was the reason that I decided to be a principal, because I felt that as an administrator I would be able to do more to empower teachers.

Ironically, it was when Linda encountered closed and nonsupportive administrators that she decided to move into administration. She was content as a teacher when she felt that she had control of her classroom and input into schoolwide decisions, but she realized that these values were not being promoted by the majority of principals. Linda, who is African American, found schools in the South to be less democratically run and more racially hierarchical.

> I had never wanted to be a principal, and the main reason that I had been content before was because I felt that I had a lot of control in my own classroom, and I had an opportunity to at least have input into decisions. I did not feel I had that when I came to this district. I think it has something to do with the mentality of the South. I also think it has something to do with the idea that there are those people who are in control, and there are people who are to be controlled. Part of it was racial, and part of it was that I am the head, and I can tell you what to do because I am your supervisor.

Easing Into Shared Governance at Harriett Wilson

Linda believes that the purpose of democratic leadership is to develop leaders and decision makers who can make "decisions which are good for the majority."

When Linda talks about teachers as leaders, she conceives of leadership as more than simply involvement in schoolwide decision making. She believes that teacher leadership involves a demand by teachers to be taken seriously as professionals. She commented on the sad state of teacher thinking:

> I really believe that teachers have been trained out of creative thinking and creative problem solving with their reliance on published materials. There's a teacher's guide that tells you exactly what you're supposed to say. There is a curriculum guide in the district that tells you what you are supposed to say, how you are supposed to say it, and how often you are supposed to say it. So, I think teachers have begun to rely so much on somebody else's creativity that

they really don't realize that they can make those decisions themselves, that they are thinkers, that they are problem solvers.

During her first year at Harriett Wilson, Linda felt that the teachers thought she could not make decisions, and this was beginning to affect her ability to lead. In hindsight, Linda feels that it was perhaps a mistake to be so democratically oriented her first year.

I don't know that it was a real good idea to come in as a democratic leader the very first year before I got a reading of the staff. There was a perception that I didn't want to make decisions, that I couldn't make decisions, that I didn't want to accept the responsibility for decisions. I think there have been some problems that would not have occurred if I had been more autocratic in some areas in the beginning and just said, "Okay, these are some decisions I'm going to make right now. I believe in democratic leadership, and as we get to know each other better, we will see in which areas more and more decision making can be shared." I think that I misjudged the staff in terms of their ability to look at the whole school. I think they were much more territorial. I can understand that now as I look back on it because there has been so much change in this school, and they didn't have any idea who I was. Now I think we are much more at the point where we can look at what's good for the whole school.

Even after teachers accepted the concept of shared governance, there was still much confusion about who makes which decisions. Recently Linda and the teachers met to set up some decision-making guidelines. They developed a list of schoolwide decisions and indicated who would have final decision-making authority for each. The list was divided into three categories: decisions made by teachers without the administration, decisions made by the administration with teacher input, and decisions made by the administration. Several teachers expressed the feeling that this recent clarification should help the process and provide a clearer understanding about the governance process at Harriett Wilson. Linda describes how this list was generated:

> Teachers said they didn't know which decisions they could make and which decisions they couldn't make. I decided to have people in grade-level meetings and liaison committees brainstorm as many decisions as they could think of. Then at the summer meeting we all went through the list we had generated. They'd call out a decision, and I'd say, "Okay, teachers can make that decision. This decision we'll make together." By the end of the meeting, we had a schoolwide decision-making list.

Instructional Leadership and Nonnegotiables

Linda acknowledges that there are still some gray areas in the group's decision making. For example, she feels that there are some general values and beliefs that are nonnegotiable, especially in the area of what constitutes effective teaching for children.

> We're going to have to use manipulatives in math. That's the way our curriculum is. I believe it is good for children, good for our particular student population. We're going to have to involve children in making decisions about their learning. We're going to have to do long-range planning. I won't say how your plans have to look or work, but you're going to have to make them; that's just good teaching. When teachers say, "Well, you know we didn't do that before," I reply, "Well, maybe you didn't do that before, but this is what we have to do now."

Linda does not feel that there is any contradiction between being a democratic leader and being an instructional leader. She feels that her democratic leadership does not imply an "anything goes" attitude toward instruction. On the contrary, as the instructional leader of the school, she feels that she has an obligation to set some broad guidelines for the teachers to follow. The extent to which the principal and the teachers reach agreement on these guidelines determines how democratic the school is. The greater the consensus on instructional issues, the easier it is for the principal to exercise instructional leadership.

> My responsibility as a principal really is to the children, and if I see areas that are ineffective, I've got to say that we're not effective here and that we have got to change. I think it's my responsibility to be an instructional leader by helping teachers make informed decisions within particular guidelines of good education.

Eliciting Teachers' Voices

Especially in her first years as a democratic leader, Linda had to brace herself to hear the criticism that her democratic approach elicited from the teachers. Linda's self-confidence and her many years of classroom experience have helped her weather the conflicts that change inevitably brings. She also has learned a few things about how to get teachers who are accustomed to closed and unsafe environments to free themselves to voice their criticisms in public.

> I don't rely on other people's assessment of me to validate who I am. I think it's really important that leaders feel a strong sense of confidence and self-worth because without that it can really be rough. They have to have a tough skin because part of being a democratic leader is being willing to listen to criticism that may be well founded or may not be well founded. They have to be able to have people point a finger at them and say, "It's your fault that things are this way. If you had only done such and such. . . . " If they can't listen to the flack that they're going to get, and they feel that they've always got to defend themselves, they're going to come off as being defensive. Leaders get a lot of respect from people when they are willing to take a frontal attack and say, "Thank you very much, I'm glad that you were able to express the way you felt."

I think you have a truly democratic environment only when you can have that type of dialogue with the principal present as well as when the principal is absent. However, I think it starts when the principal is absent. That is why in our small group meetings, I make sure I am not present initially. Some teachers can use the anonymity of the group to get out what they want to say. They begin to get used to speaking their minds, and finally they get to the point where they just freely say what they feel even in my presence.

Linda comes back repeatedly to the notion that democratic leadership is a process and that although we strive to get there, we seldom totally succeed. Being democratic is so difficult in part because we must unlearn all of the antidemocratic behaviors that we acquired in the process of our socialization.

I see that democratic leadership is a process, and we are aiming toward it. I don't see that we are there. I see that I am growing in the process of becoming a democratic leader. I think that it shouldn't be what I alone want it to be, and I need to continually get feedback on how I'm doing in order to continue in that process.

Widening the Circle

Linda is aware that parents are not formally involved in decision making at the school. Although she would like to begin putting parent representatives in the school's shared-governance groups, she is not sure the teachers are ready for this. Her current strategy is to increase parent involvement as volunteers in classrooms so as to build more trust between parents and teachers.

Right now, we have staff development on effective schools, and of course one of the components of effective schools is active parent involvement. We are increasing our volunteer programs a lot this year. When we consciously reach out and say we want to have more volunteers, then we tend to get more volunteers in the school. In this way, more and more

teachers get comfortable with having parents in their classrooms; they are then more willing to have parents involved
in helping to make decisions about what goes on in the school.

We have other parent groups. We have a very active PTA
and PTA Executive Board. We also have a local school advisory committee, which is composed of parents and teachers.
I think that we need to integrate some of those leaders into
the school leadership team instead of having separate groups,
since we're all working toward the same goals.

Recently a group of Harriett Wilson parents organized themselves and went before the school board to request a policy that would
require students to wear uniforms to school. This measure was also
supported by the teachers, but Linda was not supportive in the
beginning.

I told them in the beginning that I really didn't want uniforms but that I was here to enact the will of the community,
and eventually I was won over. It wouldn't have made any
difference though. If the parents wanted to do it, my job, I
felt, was to help them do it. I think this will encourage parents
to be even more active and involved in the school.

Linda feels that it is important to get teachers and the surround-
ing community communicating and educating each other on a regular basis, particularly in light of the current backlash from conservative groups. She feels that schools are becoming scapegoats for many
of society's ills:

I think in the last few years everybody has pointed the finger
at schools for not meeting the needs of our children, and this
has made teachers self-conscious. It has made them angry
and led them to question their own ability. It has made them
feel that they don't have control over their destinies, over
their own classrooms. They feel that the kinds of outcomes
that are going to matter are only how well children do on tests,

and not how well they do in making decisions and being able to express themselves.

I think that the responsibility of the democratic leader is to continue to provide information to teachers and to be supportive of teachers when they want to make changes which might not fit with what the external environment is saying is important. For example, right now, we're having a discussion about the merits of authentic assessment and performance-based assessment versus doing well on the standardized test.

So, I think that a democratic leader needs to be supportive of changes that the teachers want to make and fight some of the battles for them if they feel that the curriculum is not meeting the needs of the children. The principal needs to allow teachers to change and then allow them to talk about what kind of accountability measures they are going to have. In that way, the principal and the leadership team can say to the higher-ups, "Well, this is what we're doing at our school, and we are basing it on some informed decisions that we're making."

Linda sees herself as a facilitator of communication among the various school constituencies. Through this communication, she hopes to find some agreement about general principles that can be applied as broad standards to the education of children, whose needs she insists are her top priority.

Equity Issues

Although school principals are generally not known to be strong advocates for issues of social, racial, and gender equity, equity was a recurring theme for Linda. This may have something to do with the fact that 40% of students at Harriett Wilson are on free- or reduced-lunch programs and 100% of the students are African American. Although she does not use the term *at risk* for Harriett Wilson's students, she is committed to seeing that they all get the kind of rigorous and meaningful education that will make them lifelong learners.

An example of Linda's concern with equity occurred early in her teaching career, when she and her colleagues confronted the school board on its decision regarding a gifted program:

> The board decided that they wanted to have a self-contained gifted program in one school, and they chose our school. The teachers at our school said that we didn't have one because philosophically we didn't agree with it. We felt that we didn't want to have a pull-out program for all the gifted children in primary and another one in middle school, separating them from the rest of the kids all the time. We said we would like to meet gifted children's needs with some of the other things that we were doing. Then we said we weren't going to do it, and we didn't. I think that that's real empowerment, and I think the board accepted it because we weren't just saying we were not going to do something—we were saying, "Philosophically, this is what we believe."

Linda discourages student tracking of any kind at Harriett Wilson, and this comes from her tendency to apply democratic principles not only to herself and her staff but also to the students.

> We live in a democratic society, and I think that to function as citizens in a democratic society, we need to practice democracy everywhere. What would be most rewarding for me would be to see people extend the idea of democracy to the children. I would like to have children be more involved in making decisions about their learning, about what they want to learn and how they want to learn. I'd like to see teachers willing to talk with children and share their ideas. So, since I'm able to have teachers disagree with me and discuss things with me, I'll share that I'd like for them to do that with the children because children can only learn to be thinking, involved decision makers by doing those things.

Linda feels that student decision making will not only help teachers provide better and more relevant instruction, but it will help students develop a sense of who they are:

> We want students who are able to look at the facts of a situation, analyze them, and be able to come up with reasonable options and alternatives for themselves, rather than always having somebody on the outside imposing things on them. We are always imposing the parameters for how they should behave, what they should know, and how they should learn. We should make sure that they are going to be able to set up some of those guidelines for themselves, so that, in the process, they will get to know themselves better.

These democratic principles are applied to students at Harriett Wilson not only through eliciting their voice in decision making but also in making sure that students' self-esteem is not damaged through academic tracking. Several teachers are moving to heterogeneous groupings in their classrooms because, according to Linda, "we really feel that children who end up in the low reading group tend to stay in the low reading group. It's real hard to move out of the low reading group if all that you're surrounded with are poor readers."

The Costs of Democratic Leadership

Linda sees the move to shared governance as occurring on many fronts at once, with parents, teachers, students, and higher-ups all struggling with how to be more inclusive. Issues range from the trivial to the profound, and controversy and exhaustion seem to go with the territory. Democratic processes require a lot of energy to manage conflict and time to come together for discussion and decision making. Linda indicated that some of her most active teachers were recently starting to get "burned out" on the process:

> I think that there are people who have been supportive of shared governance in the past who are not supportive this

year. I think it may be that they are just feeling a lot of stress with so many things to do. This kind of decision making takes a lot of time. It takes a lot of meetings, and last year the people on the leadership team met a lot. It was a very long, intensive kind of training that we underwent last year, and I think they really, really got burned out. They are some of the people who've been real supportive in the past and who are saying this year, "You know, I don't want to do this," and "How did we decide we were going to do this anyhow?"

Linda often reiterates that democratic schooling is a process toward an ideal that is never really reached. Progress toward the ideal can be made, but there are constant setbacks. As new innovations are implemented, as new leadership cycles through the leadership team, as the work rhythms of the school year sap teachers' strength and tempers flare, and as leadership among higher-ups changes, there is always the need to regroup, to rethink things, and at times to change direction. Principals whose ultimate goal is to see their schools run like well-oiled machines should not attempt democratic leadership. The process is rarely smooth, but for Linda it is what makes her work gratifying.

I guess, for me, democratic leadership is an ideal I have. It's something that I really, really believe in. Seeing the staff move more and more to the point where they aren't in it for power, but to do the thinking themselves, is very gratifying to me. Seeing the energy that is present when there are many people involved in working together on a project or an issue is gratifying.

Clearly, Linda is very optimistic and excited about the growth of democratic schooling in the future. She argues that we live in a democratic society that is "changing and looking toward very different needs in the 21st century" and that we will eventually recognize the value of "working together" to deal with those needs. She also believes that enough momentum exists in society, particularly in business, to propel school democracy further.

Discussion Questions

1. How does Linda reconcile her role as an instructional leader, who must bring coherence to the school's instructional program, with her role as a democratic leader who must respect teachers as professionals?

2. In what ways are Linda's democratic principles applied to the students at Harriett Wilson Elementary School?

3. How does Linda try to create a safe place within the school, a place where teachers and students feel they can speak openly, even if it means criticizing the principal?

4. Discuss the relationship between democratic leadership and issues of equity.

5. Do you believe, as Linda does, that the purpose of democratic leadership is to develop leaders and decision makers who can make "decisions which are good for the majority"?

3

Teacher of Teachers

Empowerment in
an Elementary School

People keep telling me it's different to work here.

—Marcia Wallace, Principal
West Adams Elementary School

West Adams Elementary School is located in a picturesque, rural setting in the southeastern United States. Its student population is growing by 10% to 12% yearly. Socioeconomically diverse, 30% of the student population is on free- or reduced-lunch programs, and there are a significant number of middle- to upper-socioeconomic status children who are the offspring of local merchants and professionals. The all-female teaching and noncertified staff numbers 69 and is balanced between newer and more veteran teachers. Marcia Wallace, the principal at West Adams, describes the staff as professionals with "a true dedication to the children in our care." Marcia is white, in her mid-40s, and has been a principal for only 3 years. Before entering the principalship, Marcia spent 17 years in the classroom, and she credits this classroom experience as providing her with the type of trust in teachers that is conducive to a teacher empowerment model of leadership.

During Marcia's 3 years at West Adams, its teachers have implemented a whole-language instructional program and an outdoor education program; currently, they are working on an authentic assessment project. Although the progress that the West Adams staff is making is indeed impressive, the trust and interpersonal skills needed to work through problems and crises were the result of a lengthy and deliberate process of staff development.

Building Trust, Building a Team

Currently, most decision making at West Adams regarding instructional issues is done by the leadership team. Marcia does not chair the team and has one vote like every other member. After 3 years as principal in a League of Professional Schools site, she is beginning to see shared governance become part of the way things are done at West Adams. Whereas before, process issues dominated, there is now more of a "product" emerging, according to Marcia. One of the few things educational researchers know for sure is that innovations of any type work only when those involved in the innovation are trained in both technical and process skills; the teachers at West Adams have improved both their teamwork and communication skills. Marcia is reaping the benefits of this staff training:

> I'm seeing a product in terms of working together as teams. We do not need any staff development in that regard now, whereas a year to a year and a half ago we desperately needed it; we've taken care of that. We did the staff development, and we did a lot of team-building kinds of things. I can see those being used. I can also see some communication avenues becoming routine now, and we have even smoothed that and refined some ways of communicating.

> I'm glad to see it become "the way we do things" because that means we've internalized it to the point that it just happens. I see action research starting. . . . We're doing some

real good work there on issues that are of great interest to us. Leadership has emerged. People have joined, if they're interested. Groups have stabilized and now we're not so concerned with how we're doing it, but now we're really getting to focus on what we're doing.

As is predictable in shared-governance approaches, there have been periods when shared decision making has broken down. Marcia describes what she considers perhaps the lowest point in West Adams's struggle for shared governance as a school:

A year ago we had not worked together as a whole school staff, as a whole group. Grade levels had worked together, committees had worked together, and the leadership team members had worked together. But, as far as getting the whole staff together and attempting to make decisions, we hadn't tried it—not on anything that was major, those "to-the-heart" kinds of things that run very deeply with persons that are involved. So we tried to start with, "How do you rotate old leadership off and new leadership on?" It was about major decisions with a very inexperienced group, and it was an absolute disaster. Anybody in this building will tell you—I mean everybody remembers still vividly—what a mess it was. So, we looked back, we evaluated the situation, we tabled that whole concept, we admitted that we needed some more work in group dynamics, and then we sought some help. We went to the league to inquire of schools that were ahead of us by a year and had transitioned people into what they found worked and what they found not to work. Then we put our plan together and took it to the faculty. It was discussed, it was debated. A little bit of alteration was done here and there, and we walked out of the door an hour later with our method in hand. [For more on the league method, see Resource A.]

According to Marcia, what turned things around was the work the staff did on team building, their analyses of leadership styles and personality styles, and numerous retreats together. They were all able to agree that decision making could be done in three ways:

Besides making decisions within the leadership team itself, decisions can also be taken back to the whole faculty. They vote on it and make that decision within that group, or they can send it out for more study. Any time there has been anything that is going to touch upon the whole school, it has consistently gone back to the whole faculty.

More recently there was a change in the membership of the leadership team. Three members cycled off, and three new ones cycled onto the team. Marcia describes what it is like to do team rebuilding with the new membership:

Some people typically feel so much more free to talk, and, when it comes time for discussion, they are the ones who just very comfortably go on. But then we sense a little reservation, and the reservation is in a couple of the new people. And the group just doesn't have the same feel. We're just not operating quite as smoothly as the group that disbanded, the group that was operating toward the latter part of last year, but that group had worked together for 3 years. It reminds me very much of the original leadership team 4 years ago, even a year before we were in the league, and we had our very first leadership team. I think what we need to do is look at this group as perhaps not as undeveloped as that original group, but certainly not as a highly developed group. What I'm trying to say is that I've noticed developmental stages, and now it's starting to repeat. It appears that way every time we seat a new group. We anticipated that to a degree, but I guess we also thought we'd have instant camaraderie within the new group. It is getting better, but I see that we're going to have to repeat with this group some development things the other group had long mastered.

Parents and the community are not generally part of decision making at West Adams except through the Parent Teacher Organization (PTO) executive board, which has teacher, parent, and administrative representation but is limited to an advisory role and only in noninstructional areas. Marcia admits that she is not sure "if you asked every parent in the school that they'd have a clue about the democratic leadership that goes on."

Decision Making in
Instructional and Noninstructional Arenas

Marcia Wallace makes a clear distinction between instructional and noninstructional arenas of decision making. She believes that teachers are most likely to give the time and energy required for participatory decision making in those areas that bear most directly on their classrooms, so she involves teachers in making decisions about instructional issues. Although she acknowledges the system's limits, she also insists that teachers become actively involved in schoolwide instructional decisions:

> I think the primary purpose in democratic leadership would be to offer professional people the opportunity to perform in a professional manner. I don't say that just because I'm the principal or because I need to have a dictatorial kind of situation. The teachers are the people that are trained to teach, and they should be allowed to practice their profession. I understand there are parameters; the system puts parameters on me regarding the building and how we will operate, but there's also flexibility within those parameters. And I think giving teachers a voice in how we're going to operate allows them to excel at their profession.

Besides the success of the children at West Adams, Marcia's greatest satisfaction in being a principal is seeing teachers grow professionally, or as she puts it, "seeing a staff that's anxious to come back in August." Because she feels strongly about teacher involvement in decision making, she screens teacher candidates during interviews to make sure she will get teachers who do not expect an authoritarian principal.

> When I interview a person, I will not hesitate to ask the question, "Who or what group of people do you think should be

making the instructional decisions in the building?" And if they look at me and say, "Oh, you, because you're the principal," that doesn't say they're a bad teacher, it just says maybe they're not going to be real happy right here at this particular school.

There is a certain irony in this, because Marcia does not include teachers in personnel decisions. According to Marcia, teachers prefer that she do the hiring. They claim that it is a noninstructional, managerial task that they do not want to be involved in.

> They absolutely do not want to become involved in that [personnel decisions]. They much prefer that I keep that strictly in the realm of work I do. They consider it one of the managerial kinds of things, and I'm very comfortable with that. However, I feel like I know the staff well, and I know the way they work, so I try to look for people who are going to be compatible. But I'm sure all people, all principals do that. They want to have a staff that's going to have harmony. It makes everybody's work much easier.

This division between instructional and noninstructional aspects of school life is a common theme at West Adams. There seems to be a strict line drawn between the world inside and outside the classroom. Teachers are protected from incursions from outside their classrooms but also deprived of leadership in areas that might indirectly affect their work in classrooms. This seems to be a pragmatic teaching staff that wants to protect their time and essentially trusts the principal to make some decisions for them.

Besides personnel, there are other areas in which teachers do not participate, such as the general management of the physical plant. Marcia is not afraid to borrow ideas from other principals who have more experience than she, and the "minding of the mansion" team was the result of this sharing of ideas among principals:

> It was an idea that I picked up from another principal in another school system, and it made good sense. She had a managerial team that was called the minding of the mansion

team. Those people who participated in that group had a function of keeping that building operative so the teachers could do what they were hired to do, and that's teach.

I now have a group like that, and we meet every other Friday. My head custodian, my cafeteria manager, my secretary, the instructional lead teacher, and I sit down. That's when we plan. It's also a time when I can check for some routine repetitive kinds of things like, Do we need more toilet paper? Is it time to order? Do we need to do anything differently here in the cafeteria? We have Grandparents Week coming up, so we need to get geared up for having lots of additional people in the school. Well, that means grocery orders are going to change. Staff members who clean the cafeteria are going to have to work longer when we finish serving, and teachers are going to need to be informed because it's going to delay everybody's lunch. This is a time when I can pick through those kinds of things that otherwise I could be going all over this building trying to attend to.

Marcia accomplishes two important things through these meetings; she gets input from her staff and saves herself the job of, as she puts it, "going all over this building" contacting everyone.

An example of Marcia's streamlined approach to democracy is evident in her handling of duty-free lunch periods. Recently the state legislature passed a statute that teachers would not be required to do lunch duty. Marcia saw this as a noninstructional issue and did not include teachers in related decisions. She did, however, get input from another sector:

We were exploring what to do with duty-free lunch here in the county. I picked up the phone, and I instantly knew everything that Barbara [a fellow league principal] knew that was going on, and nobody knows better than Barbara about some real innovative ways that people have approached this duty-free lunch. I considered duty-free lunch a noninstructional issue, so I dealt with it; the leadership team didn't. I needed input from the mansion team regarding how we could do this. I then dictatorially said, "There will not be lunches eaten elsewhere in this school for the following reasons." For the most part that wasn't a problem.

Marcia admits to making unilateral decisions fairly often and explains that in doing so she must feel comfortable that her decision is the best one for the school as a whole. Another example she gives, like the personnel decisions discussed above, seems to blur the line between instructional and noninstructional matters:

> If I needed to make a change within a team of teachers, if something is not working the way I feel it ought to, or if there's not smooth collaboration, then it may be that a person or persons needed to be moved by me into a different grade level. There they might work better because of philosophy or something like that.

Marcia has high credibility with teachers not only because she has inspired trust but also because she is known as a fine classroom teacher. In fact, she occasionally steps in for teachers and conducts class for them. This may help explain why teachers seem to defer decisions, many of which have implications for their classrooms, to Marcia. Marcia and the teachers trust each other when it comes to instructional issues. Marcia even feels there is a connection between classroom experience and the kind of trust from teachers that is a prerequisite for democratic leadership:

> I think that the longer you have spent in the classroom, the more likely you are to subscribe to democratic leadership, mostly because you have trust for teachers in general.

This classroom connection is a common theme in how Marcia defines democratic leadership. In her mind, as well as in the minds of many others, democratic leadership is associated with more holistic and process approaches to instruction. This leads Marcia to conclude that for democratic leadership to prevail, new forms of student assessment must be promoted. She reasons that innovations take time, and if they are judged too quickly based on standardized test scores, schools will be less likely to take risks.

> I think we're going to have to be very careful that it's [democratic leadership] not allowed to be construed as a fad. I think we're going to have to be very careful that the democratic work that is being done in schools is assessed in the appropriate fashion. I'm speaking of comprehensive assessment, authentic assessment, and portfolio assessment. I don't think that we should have to be held to answer only to standardized test scores; there's a lot more to assessing a child than that. And I think that educators who are managed in a democratic fashion believe that. I know we believe that, as a school. Test scores are fine. We know we're accountable to a degree, but don't praise and don't hang us because our test scores are such and such. I'm saying that even though we've generally been at the top within the system. But I don't think it's fair to assess children only by test scores. It's much less fair to assess the quality of work being done by teachers by test scores. And I'm fearful that innovation takes time. You have to avoid fear and to have that risk-free environment to go ahead and experiment.

Extending Democracy to Students

Marcia explains that at West Adams they are also trying to extend democracy to students, both in the form of participation in decision making and in addressing equity issues of at-risk students. Recently when an itinerant art teacher came in for a few days to teach a unit on Native American art, the students indicated that they would like him to be invited back. This turned into an exercise in democracy, which Marcia describes:

> When it was time to evaluate him, we asked the children, "Does Mr. Chamblis need to come back, and does he need to stay longer?" Well, this year he came for 2 whole months. I try to make a point of letting the students know when I am

using their input. We were fortunate because we received a local grant that paid his fee, with enough money left over that we could buy a real tepee, which we ordered for the school. Now, that sounds silly, but that's outdoor instructional space. You can put 40 children in this tepee and teach. That gets their attention.

So, anyway, they have learned from Mr. Chamblis how symbols are placed on tepees. They have learned that never would one family of Native Americans copy another family's tepee design—that is completely improper. They've learned what symbols mean for different things.

We ended up with suggestions from the children about purchasing our tepee. It was made for us. Our posts came in from Montana. And one of our classes did overhead transparencies with the three top designs. They took it to every class in this school, and the children and teachers voted. All in all the children had more votes for their design than the faculty members. Then the design was painted on the tepee by a class, by our little self-contained special education class. So, we had a tepee dedication on field day as the opening ceremony. That is student participation. The children know they have ownership in that tepee, and they refer to it as our tepee, like it is our school.

Some democratic instructional arrangements are used at West Adams to promote student equity. In the early grades whole language and heterogeneous grouping are used so as not to stigmatize students. Then, from third grade on, students are tracked by reading and math levels. The tracking system, however, builds in extra time and attention for those who need it.

We do "skills groups" for language arts and math from third grade on up. And we have let our faster-moving skills groups and our good, solid, on-grade-level skills groups run with a few more kids in there. The very strongest teachers on the team are volunteering to take the slower-moving skills groups, and we're cutting those numbers to no more than a dozen children in a class.

Action Research

Some of the innovations that the West Adams staff has engaged in are the result of action research. Although action research is one of the emphases of the League of Professional Schools, few schools have used it extensively, particularly in the first few years of restructuring. The staff at West Adams, however, has found it helpful to have data to aid in problem solving. Marcia describes some current action research projects:

> We are studying "resetting the clock," we call it. It's about how an instructional year is put together from time frame or different perspectives. We're putting that issue in our action research. We are also studying retention in order to seek alternatives to retention, and we're looking at it as a case study by case study, child by child; for the most part our student population is stable enough that we can do that. We want to take it right through middle school. You know, if it appears successful to avoid retention in elementary, is it still considered successful in seventh grade or does something change? We're also looking at a multiage grouping, and we're studying conflict resolution right now, too.

External Obstacles
to Democratic Leadership

Like so many other principals who are trying to democratize their institutions within largely hierarchical and authoritarian systems, Marcia is frustrated by certain central-office decisions. Although central-office administrators are supportive in theory, their behaviors are often out of sync with their espoused theories. For example, a new wing for Marcia's school was recently designed without her input. However, the last superintendent was generally supportive, and the one who has just been hired promises to be supportive as well.

> We are in a period of change within our system. Obviously, 4 years ago, the feeling was that principals needed input from staff, and that's why the leadership teams were insisted upon. I guess I don't need to tell you that in some buildings they are simply a rubber stamp, while in other buildings they drive decision making. And probably there are in-betweens to those extremes. Probably some are moving more smoothly than others.

> We've just gotten a new superintendent, and the shared-governance concept has been in the past supported by the now retired superintendent. The county office supported us in that they paid fees for the league, supported us in some attempts that we made to do things a little differently than other people, and there have been several occasions where we have applied for a variance on a given issue and it has been granted. For example, a year ago we applied for a variance to, of all things, the school calendar, which I considered a major issue. I mean, the school calendar is board approved, and that's a biggie. We wrestled with this idea of what we felt we needed to do in staff development, as well as the urgency with which we wanted to do it. The faculty felt we needed to be back at school a day early, but not just as volunteers, as paid professionals. And so with the creative power that lies within this staff, we came up with an alternative to the school calendar, which was to come back a day early, have the staff development, and then during February staff development, which is systemwide, West Adams staff stayed home. The group supported it.

Another promising sign is the fact that teachers and community members were included on the hiring committees for the new superintendent:

We were asked by the Board of Education to have representation on a search committee. Now they did not actually
go out and search, but they did meet the finalists. I think it
was two, possibly three finalists that our group met with,
and it was very community based. Each school had a representative. We elected ours, but some principals put themselves on the committee! I thought that was real interesting,
but our staff felt that it needed to be an elected person. I told
the staff that it was up to them to decide, if they felt I needed
to be the person, fine. But if they felt we needed to elect
someone, that was fine too. We were going to do it the way
the staff felt we should. And so they chose to elect. The person
that became a member of the committee knew, of course, the
importance of hiring someone who believes in a shared
decision-making philosophy. And I am hearing from the
people on that committee that, yes, that is something that
this person does believe in.

Another critical variable besides the central-office personnel is
the attitudes of one's administrative colleagues in the district. A
common complaint of democratic principals is the fact that they
must be careful not to offend other principals in the district who may
not share a democratic view of administration. Democratic principals are often in the classic "damned if you do, damned if you don't"
position. If the district does not support democratic leadership, then
they must keep a low profile; if the district does support it, then they
are often held up as an example and perceived by other principals
as having special favor with the superintendent. Recently Marcia
was asked to give a presentation at a district principals' meeting and
she could feel resentment coming from some of her colleagues:

The audience was my colleagues, and some saw it as a distrac-
tion. They made a couple of comments before we even got
into the building like, "Well, I guess we'll find out all of the
answers from you today, Marcia." I noticed little things that,
maybe, being the feeling person that I am, I perceived incor-
rectly. Sharon and I, that's my lead teacher, copresented. Inter-

estingly enough, we sensed that it may be difficult. I think there was a degree of resentment or something going on, and it wasn't real comfortable.

Because of this resentment, Marcia often does not choose to share with other administrators the innovative things the teachers at West Adams are doing for fear it will be viewed as bragging.

I know when to keep my mouth shut. I don't talk about how we operate. For instance, the chapter one model. We can either adopt the generic model that the system has put together, or we can put something together and submit it and it would be considered. Then we may get it and then we may not. Again, the whole staff put it together. We've been studying our remedial services and we came up with a plan, and we turned it in. I didn't ask anybody else how they came up with theirs. I didn't tell anybody else how we came up with ours.

Marcia's remarks also reflected cautiousness about the future of democratic schooling. As noted, she had deep worries that it might be construed as a fad if it was not "assessed in the appropriate fashion." She argued that too much emphasis on standardized test scores rather than other forms of assessment (e.g., portfolio assessment) could destroy people's willingness to do the necessary research and experimentation required to continue to learn "to search for what's best for children . . . what really works."

Marcia's approach to democratic leadership, although limited in many ways, shows a consistent concern with children and classrooms as the central focus of the school. She has made some pragmatic decisions about when to include staff in decision making and what areas to keep off-limits. Parents and students are not actively involved in decision making within the school on a regular basis, but now that Marcia has the leadership team running more or less smoothly, she can give more attention to extending democracy to other constituencies. As is the case with all administrators attempting to extend democratic principles in their schools, there are numerous potential obstacles from both within the school and without.

Discussion Questions

1. What is the difference between "teacher empowerment" and "democratic leadership"? Which best describes Marcia's approach to leadership?

2. How do you feel about Marcia's distinction between decision making in instructional and noninstructional areas?

3. How does Marcia link her views about empowering teachers to the empowerment of students? Parents?

4. Using Marcia's case as an example, what are some of the major obstacles to exercising democratic leadership in schools?

5. Use Marcia's case to discuss whether a principal can make unilateral decisions and still maintain credibility as a democratic leader.

4

Tough Love

Loyalty, Commitment, and Challenge in a Predominantly African American Middle School

I can't think of anything that I wouldn't do for this school. It's just a challenge that I've had, and that burning is in here, that love is in here. I love this particular level. I've had several opportunities to leave here, but I'm not ready to leave.

—James Wooley, Principal
Grady Middle School

Genial, smooth, professional, and businesslike, James Wooley sits in an office decorated with awards and recognitions received by him personally and by the school. Presiding over Grady Middle School has been his personal challenge for 15 years. The school's students are predominantly low socioeconomic status and 73% African American. The faculty is 74% white, prepared in middle school teaching, and described by James as supportive, cooperative, and unquestioningly committed. The school is situated in a large, rural county comprised mostly of pine forest and swamp, with unemployment reaching 7% and per capita income a mere $7,300. Grady Middle School has an aura of being greatly used with a need for refurbishing but is kept adequately clean and neat.

James's ascent to this position at Grady was swift. After teaching high school social studies for 4 years, he then entered graduate school with the goal of earning a degree in guidance and counseling. But, as he put it, he "didn't have much choice about becoming a principal." It was "a city-county, black-white" issue. Integration had begun, with myriad attendant racial tensions and incidents, and newspaper reports included fabricated stories biased against the school in which James would soon become a leader; he was asked—as a black man—to "help us with the black kids, okay?" Targeted for the assistant principalship, James accepted the discipline-oriented job in the high school. Within a year, he was promoted to middle school principal and moved to Grady, where he has remained in the same position for 15 years. During our interview, James recalled his first days as an administrator:

> The first thing I saw when I came here was chaos. I mean, kids were all over the place, and teachers were doing whatever they wanted to do. I felt like I had to get control of the situation! To make a long story short, it took things like walking down the hall with a paddle, spanking a kid's behind right there in front of everybody.

According to James, the school had a "bad reputation" because it was located in an African American neighborhood, across from a housing project, and it had an African American student population and an African American administrator:

> I felt I had the majority of the teachers wanting the best school possible, and there's no way I could personally achieve that. But a lot of them felt as I did, that we were a sort of secondhand citizen. We did not get the respect in the community, not as professionals or as a school. So, it might be a little bit up in the clouds, but we kind of went off on a mission to make this the best school we could ever have right here.

We've got a lot of black kids here, a lot of them from poor families. But they're no different than any other children. They need to be taught, they need to be loved, they need to be understood. You've got to give them a chance. Just because they approach you in a certain way, or their tone might be a little louder than other students, doesn't mean that they're being disrespectful to you.

After starting out with such serious disadvantages, James quickly developed a protective stance. For example, he brooks no disloyalty to the school:

I say, "Don't ever let me hear you out in public running us down. I don't like gossip. Gossip can't walk, it has to be carried. And if there's something you don't like, sit down and talk with me about it. If you work here you're going to be loyal to this organization, and if you ever have to question my loyalty, then you don't have to worry about me working for you." I'm not trying to be a rebel, but if I'm working at a job, at a profession, and I don't put everything in it that needs to be put in it, then I'm not doing my job.

A Change of Course

Thus deciding that he wanted to "turn this thing around," James spent the next 10 years, by his calculations, doing just that. "I'd liken it to a large ship in a channel, in making that turn," he remarked. By many indicators, that has happened, albeit slowly. In recent years, Grady Middle School has repeatedly won state awards for excellence; one student won the state spelling bee; students won district, state, and regional science awards; and even the cafeteria won awards. James wanted Grady Middle School to be a school where people sent their kids "because of the education, not the location or because of it being perceived to be a, quote, black school." And yet, James still feels the sting of criticism because "being black in America . . . we have to be twice as good to be considered half as good."

By now, he is perceived by many in the community as a disciplinarian who influences both students and parents by his "fairness and honesty," as reported in a recent newspaper article. Although he may see unfairness in this world, he is determined to make a difference for others—a position that everyone respects.

James's philosophy carries with him a personal conviction, a pride that comes from being a graduate of this same school and a philosophy that carries him through hard times.

> It goes back to some of my old teachers. Their philosophy was, "No matter what you're given, James, do it." I had to take tickets at games, hold classes in the shop, and, you know, no matter what is asked of you, you just do it. That's just our upbringing. As the prophet says, "You don't know what's going to come out of this."

This philosophy has been deeply reflected in James's hiring practices. From the start, he wanted to recruit and hire people who could work with him, something he admits is not necessarily easy.

> I demand a lot. I demand total loyalty, although it might not sound democratic. I have pulled a staff together that is willing, able, and ready; they are committed to taking a child from where we find him and educating him from that point. I ask my people to "give me everything you've got plus some, and I'm not going to settle for 100%; your commitment to me is going to be 125%." No, nobody ever reaches that, but that's the commitment.

James also derives great satisfaction from nurturing people and supporting their development:

> Seeing people grow is gratifying. To touch on one gratifying thing, it's that I trained a lot of assistant principals, and I gave them a lot of responsibility and authority. I had confidence in them, as I do the teachers.

For James, interviewing for a job at Grady Middle School is an intense and serious business, perhaps his most important responsibility. "Being an excellent teacher and being able to work with children are two different things," he proclaims. He announces that he selects on "gut feeling," yet his interview protocol includes some 160 questions on a candidate's background, philosophy, and instructional approach. He looks for sympathy as well as empathy for students, an understanding that a certain child may be just barely capable of getting to school and a heavy homework assignment for that child is unreasonable, for example. James focuses on interpersonal relationships in his interviews, and he looks in particular at a candidate's experience with minority children. He also reports that he "keeps drilling, just keeps hammering at what I want, that commitment." Later, after the teacher has joined the faculty, James is likely to analyze his or her disciplinary referrals.

In turn, James recognizes the talents and capabilities of others: "getting myself into the background because I'm bashful, and because I see in others things that I don't have." James wants to give teachers a lot of responsibility, as well as the authority to go with it, to "not smother people." He criticizes indecision and pushes faculty members to "think, brainstorm, work among themselves, and take the chance to grow and develop." As a result, he proudly announces, several of the school's teachers have gone on to become principals and directors.

A Democratic Leader?

What is democratic about James's approach? Can such a strong, confident, authoritarian (in some respects) leader operate democratically? James's response to this question was interesting:

> I cannot be uncomfortable with who I am, and I cannot worry about what people say or about people who might challenge me. It's no problem for me to say, "Tell me if you're doing something that's enhancing in the class." I don't always have the best ideas, and I've never been so insecure that I could not or would not listen to the ideas of other people.

Even before we got into empowerment, which is being able to make decisions in terms of curriculum and instruction, I asked people for their input; if we disagreed, we disagreed behind closed doors.

As James sees it, input from teachers and parents is the key, and support for trial and error comes next:

The purpose is to provide a forum, if you will, for people to share in the operation of the school. When people have ownership they tend to put a little bit more into it. The only thing I say is "Try," and I would be upset if a person didn't try. Nine times out of 10 I will allow you to do what you need to do. I have confidence in them to handle the job. If you fail, so what? Let's go back, and let's revamp it. I figure I can get more good out of people who continue to try things and fail (but are supported by me) rather than to ridicule them. And I have never been the kind of principal to stand over one's shoulder; I try to provide a sense of freedom. I try to give people an opportunity to feel good about where they work and to contribute.

This view is exemplified in James's comments about the future of schooling in America:

Democratic schooling is the wave of the future. Principals are going to have to allow teachers more input. We can't have an authoritarian saying, "This is the way we're going to do it." Not that there isn't a place for some of that because you obviously have to have direction and to give direction, but I don't think we're going to be able to sit back and allow that type of leadership to prevail. And we're just going to have to involve parents. If we're going to prepare kids for the 21st century, a global economy, we're going to have to allow them more input too.

James's acceptance of risk and experimentation has paid off. Indeed, the statewide shared-governance on-site facilitators' reports include allusions to group decision making around issues of instructional equipment and climate or morale at Grady Middle School. Several instructional initiatives grew out of the efforts of faculty members through their representatives in liaison groups. These have included, in recent years, alternative classes for at-risk students, academic-recognition programs, special projects for specific populations of students, project-oriented curricula, and cooperative-learning activities. All of this is an overlay to the middle school concept enacted several years ago with block scheduling and teaming as its basic premise. Teachers are increasingly being given the freedom and the responsibility to be creative and dedicated to find activities appropriate for their students. Furthermore, teachers have collected data by conducting action research in their classrooms and recently have determined their staff development needs. (For information about action research methods, see Calhoun, 1994.)

In turn, James unflaggingly does several things that contribute to the increasing stability of Grady's faculty and staff. He reports that he is always there to take care of the faculty and staff, which "sounds kind of fluffy, but that's the relationship." He also matches new teachers with mentors,

> to put them with someone who's been here, who knows my style, and what I'm after. I ask the mentor to give them all the advantages and all the pitfalls, and after a time the new person knows they can come to me if they want to.

Unusual Approaches

James is also determined to do whatever it takes to run the school "legally, ethically, and morally." On at least one occasion, he has stood up against the superintendent, doing what he felt was best for the school. James even disclosed a touch of subversive activity on his part:

> I can't say that I always follow all the Board of Education rules. . . . They're not always in the best interest of this particular school. I sometimes have to challenge the rules, but not

in a vicious or malicious way. I can't sit here and tell you that I always followed the directives of the superintendent. I've had to change some things, but when the reports go down there, yes, the reports say exactly what they want them to say. But my number one obligation is to this school, and I don't mind taking a risk if it means I'm going to be able to improve education for the kids I've got. I also broke a state department rule about pulling out a teacher in reading. I had a little tiff with the lady from the state department but she finally conceded, and what I did has become a model for other districts.

Similarly, knowing that his presence creates undue influence on teachers during voting at faculty meetings, James often leaves the room. "If I have made a previous statement in favor of something, for example, and it calls for a vote, they're going to vote for it," he admitted. We wondered if James ever countermands the teachers' instructionally oriented decisions, particularly those derived from shared-governance processes and their related voting or decision making. Apparently so: When he felt that some teachers, out of laziness and a reluctance to prepare for class, supported a decision regarding teaching reading in the content area, James spoke with the department chairperson, saying he "detected something wrong." "In terms of curriculum and instructional matters, I give leeway, but I'm looking for results," James noted. He told the chairperson:

Even though you have taken a vote on it, and even though this is not necessarily democratic, I am being honest with you. I want you to take another hard look at it. If we're not going to do it for the best interests of the school, then I'm not going to be party to it. My criterion is whether it's going to benefit the school. I'm willing to take a chance on basically anything, but that's where I step forward.

On another occasion, however, faculty resistance to a project was all James needed to back off:

As I remember, we were involved in a lot of different activities at that time. I realized they felt kind of swamped, and I
accepted that. There was no bitterness. But I came back to it
at another point, and they said, "We're ready for it now."

However, for all his blend of pushing and supporting, stepping
out of the limelight and stepping forward to assert himself gently,
James has been known to force an issue or two.

One of my goals was to reduce the use of the textbook. In
essence I said, "No textbooks." Now I realize that was a bit
far-flung. The teachers said, "We're going to make a thousand
copies because he said we can't use textbooks." So I said,
"You're not going to use the copier." So they asked me, "Can
we buy our own copier, if we raise the money?" It was not
a high-speed copier, and I said "no" to using the school copier.
My point was to challenge them to come up with a different
way of doing things; they had used books as a crutch. They
still use textbooks and some of them did better than others
developing their own plans. And now they've decided they
would make six interdisciplinary units, and they have common planning time to do it.

Parental involvement is high on James's list of priorities. In fact,
he was inclined to extend one student's suspension for fighting from
2 to 5 days, for the express purpose of getting the parent's attention.
And he steadfastly refuses to grant extra privilege to privileged
students, as in the case of the son of a state official:

I have a standard rule. If you fight, you go home. I don't care
who it is, what color, you can be polka-dot. I don't see any
exceptions. The father couldn't give me a good reason why
I should break my rule. Now, years ago someone told me
that I was discriminating against the black and prejudiced
against the white, and I said, "That puts me exactly where I
want to be." I have told parents, "If you will give me a day
in this school, I will lift that suspension." So I've had parents

come out and spend a day with their children, and it's much worse on that child having that parent shadow them around all day.

Inner Workings

What makes James tick? "I don't know," he says, "I just do." But digging a little deeper, it seems his mother was most influential:

> I never knew my father, and I remember in fourth grade ... I got disturbed because some kids said some things. My mother said, "You're getting along better without a father than most children do with one." That was a turning point in my life. It propelled me to go on. My mother sacrificed for me. She was a "driver," but people felt they could come to her, could talk to her.

After telling us about his self-effacing tendency to silently grab the nearest seat—within 10 feet of the door—when he arrives at school functions, this strong leader even confesses to his own personal sort of stage fright:

> Number one, I don't like speaking before groups. I'm relatively shy and bashful, and I don't like public recognition. The night before the first day of preplanning is my worst night. The first day I walk in that door prepared and I've half-slept and I'm there at 7:00 (for an 8:00 meeting) and it's stressful. I try to be the first one in there so I won't have to walk in.

James Wooley is a strong administrator who takes his responsibility seriously, almost as a special calling or mission. Blending authority with political realism, he continues to lead at Grady Middle School.

Discussion Questions

1. What contextual elements may have influenced James Wooley's philosophy and approach to educational leadership?

2. Whose vision—that of James Wooley, the teachers, the parents, the students, or a combination of all of these—is enacted at Grady Middle School?

3. What procedures or policies appear to be in place that facilitate shared decision making between faculty and staff at Grady Middle School?

4. What primary barriers inhibit further efforts to democratize Grady Middle School? What factors might enhance such efforts? How have James's hiring practices influenced these efforts?

5. What positive or negative effects has racial discord had on efforts to develop this school?

6. Do you note evidence of authentic collegiality among faculty members at Grady Middle School? Do you note any evidence of coercion or authoritarianism on the part of the leader? Discuss your responses.

5

Matchmaker

Initiating Democratic Schooling in a Large High School

*I've always wanted my faculty to share in everything, the good
and the bad. I've always wanted them to have a voice, because when
you have a voice in things it makes a difference. It makes you want
to work harder, and it makes you want to be successful. I try to praise
people and provide opportunities for them. This is the focal point.*

—Loretta Ford, Principal
Kennedy High School

Four years ago, Loretta Ford became principal of Kennedy High
School, a rural county school of 2,100 students and 120 faculty
and staff members. Her manner is clearly professional, yet she is comfortably dressed. An African American woman, Loretta is a native
of Pitt County, where Kennedy is located. She welcomed us to her
slightly cluttered, very homelike office. Plants, a rocking chair, personal decorations, and current magazines match Loretta's warm voice
and grandmotherly approach. She laughs easily as we talk, and it is
clear that she loves working with this low socioeconomic status,
highly mobile community. She also took us on a tour of the older brick

facility, which is traditionally decorated with green paint and tile floors.

It is clear that Loretta considers herself an educator first and an administrator second. We asked her what nudged her toward democratic leadership rather than toward a more authoritarian style, and she readily shared the following:

> I think it goes according to the situation. There might be situations in which you have to develop an authoritarian personality, but I would rather see a person be more in the middle of the road. If you are totally authoritarian, people will begin to rebuff you, and you will not be supported. This wouldn't even give your "plan" a chance.

> To be democratic, you have to let . . . people develop. I can go back to my own high school, not so much my principal but my teachers who impacted me. They were developing me, you see. They weren't saying, "O.K., you've got to do, do, do as I'm saying." They were simply permitting me to develop, and I want every teacher here to develop to his or her fullest. If I'm going to be the person to corral you and say, "It's got to be this way," then I'm not letting you develop.

But allowing people to develop seems to go hand-in-hand with sharing the decision making, as Loretta defines democratic leadership:

> I know there is something better for the whole student body than my telling you, "This is how it ought to be." I don't know everything. We would never have gotten to assessing kids differently if it were not for shared governance. We had task forces study it, and it opened doors. We're now trying things that we would never have tried before.

Loretta's philosophy of permitting others to develop is undoubtedly a freeing approach, but we wondered how she initiated democratic, shared-governance processes at Kennedy High School. Several of her comments gave us some insight into the processes of planning, challenging, and exchanging ideas for growth:

> When I came to Kennedy, I felt the faculty expected me to come with "a plan." It was probably a mistake on the part of my training that even I felt that I was supposed to come with a plan for the year. There has to be a plan, yes, but everybody has to be a part of the plan, everybody has to be involved in it.
>
> At the same time, being democratic doesn't mean that you are doing your own thing. Being democratic isn't easy. It's something you have to work at constantly. You have to make sure everybody feels comfortable. I would constantly talk to teachers and say "How do you feel about this, . . . Are you being challenged?"
>
> Some people maybe found it easy to say, "Just tell us what we're supposed to do." They want you to do something as simple as that. For example, we had an issue with the exam schedule. It was a big, hard task for us, but we came up with one answer and then we shot holes in that. "You are the principal," they said, "just tell us. We're going to do what you say to do." I even had teachers come to me and say, "I'm just tired of all this carrying on. Just get on the intercom, or just write to us and say, 'this is how it's going to be.'" But it can't be that way in a democratic school. So we went through all the trials. And then when it was all said and done, everybody said, "We feel good!" It took us several days, but everybody felt good. It was the idea of exchanging ideas, of dialoguing, of discussing, of being challenged, of wanting to change, of not being afraid to change, or afraid that if you make a mistake, you can't try something else. We decided to just keep it moving.

Thus, to Loretta, a plan, a challenge, and fearless dialogue are essential to the beginning of democratic governance in schools.

Empowerment at Kennedy
High School: The First 2 Years

Soon after becoming the principal at Kennedy, Loretta had the opportunity to attend a shared-governance conference. She brought several faculty members with her, who later enjoyed visiting and observing a shared-governance school. They learned how to arrange random, representative liaison groups that report to an all-school executive council of faculty and staff members. This firsthand experience provided the impetus for initiating shared decision-making, or shared-governance, processes at Kennedy.

> We just knew that this was exactly what all of us had been waiting for. We came back and told our faculty about it. They liked it. But at that time everyone was talking about effective schools in a different sense, so they weren't certain about shared governance, but the more they talked about it, the more opportunities they saw, the more they said, "That sounds great!" They no longer wanted things to be top-down; they said "Let's try it," and so we did.

During that first year of trial and error, facilitators from the statewide League of Professional Schools conducted an on-site observation of the democratic processes at Kennedy High School. They noted that faculty members were fairly consistent in their belief in the shared-governance operating style at Kennedy; the faculty had experienced genuine interest in their input on the part of the administration and felt pleased with some resulting changes.

Facilitators also conducted a needs assessment and identified several key areas they wanted to address. These included important academic matters such as curricula, student achievement, program development, climate, and morale. They noted a high priority on discipline and some concerns regarding absenteeism and tardiness. Staff and faculty input was solicited and used during that year on items such as the senior breakfast, the Christmas dance, miniworkshops, parent conference times, and liaison-meeting times.

However, during that first year, faculty seemed to have "too much on the table" at one time, so initially they had difficulty focusing on the admittedly important academic matters. Also, there was an absence of empirical data supporting the faculty's stated view that it was becoming easier to implement change. Even so, faculty members reported a sense of having a united voice, thus making it easier to get what they needed. The optimism and hope among faculty members were evident, even though academic matters had not yet been addressed thoroughly.

During the second year of shared governance and democratic operations at Kennedy High School, the facilitators' reports cited the low-impact issues that were dominating faculty and staff efforts. The facilitators suggested that the faculty identify a single significant issue or concern, work together toward a solution, and then implement it carefully. Concurrent with this advice was a suggestion that administrators clarify their roles and, in fact, decide what power they were comfortable giving up.

As they struggled to find time for collaboration to develop a database and to address high-impact issues in a systematic way, the faculty and staff at Kennedy High School also realized a need to build trust among themselves. A 3-day retreat at a resort area was viewed as productive and worthwhile for all who attended. Feeling that she had an advantage in being at a "smaller" high school (smaller than the one of 4,000 she recently visited), Loretta worked hard to develop a family feeling among the faculty, staff, and students. She firmly believes that "connectedness" creates an opportunity to improve a school:

> I think that one problem is that you usually don't get to know each other personally. I'm not an office person, I'm a hall person, and I like to know the students. I like parents. I like for the faculty to have retreats and for teachers to get to know their children and their grandchildren. I like the warm family effect that is generated from a smaller group. You really have to have that human touch, that human feeling. You have to know that someone's not going to slam a door in your face and make you feel like you're an isolated person, or not a real human being. I think this is what we're missing a lot of times from schools—that kind of touch.

Loretta's Development

Indeed, Loretta came by that personal approach (as well as her interest in education) honestly. A longtime resident (and native) of the county, she recalled growing up there with her family and learning to work hard, support others, and value an education:

My mother was a teacher, and my aunt was also a teacher. My first teaching experience was in elementary school. Having to work with little children, I learned to be patient and understanding and tolerant. I had heard that all along in my growing up. My father was a plasterer by trade, a very proud person. He made sure I learned to give praise where praise is due. He was highly respected and creative. In those days it was not sheetrock, it was "decorative walls," and everything had to be just right. People praised him for his work. In my family, if things weren't done well, you were encouraged.

Knowing about the struggles of having to work at things has always been a part of us. My brother and I even went to my mother's graduation from college; I was about 14, and I remember her taking classes to complete her teaching certificate. Having these goals was always a part of my background.

It was always my father's desire that my brother and I have the best education possible. He went to work in Nashville and passed Fisk University going to his job every day. And he would always say, "When my daughter grows up, I would like her to go to Fisk University." It turned out that was where I went. So I guess it was my mother and my father, my family, that instilled certain things in us that are responsible for the way I am today. Even my religious training, perhaps, played a part in my development. I've always worked in every part of the church.

I remember my high school principal; he was authoritarian—his style, his personality. I wouldn't say that the school could

not have operated in any other way, but everyone knew
what their task was. You knew what you were supposed to
do, and you did it. This was an all-black school, and he was
a black administrator. Coupled with that was the fact that
you knew you had to do things right because you were proud
of your race, and there was no playing around. That was it.
In those days, you had more parental control. If someone
didn't do something, they called your parent. The parent got
on you, and you got it. It was taken care of. He was a fine
administrator, and I went back to thank him for the things I
learned incidentally from him.

Loretta became a high school teacher, always remembering the
little boys and girls she had worked with at church; when those same
children came to her English class in high school, she realized that
they were stronger readers, in part, because of her early work with
them. She became a department chairperson, but because she felt a
little fearful of working with adults, she began taking courses in
leadership. Soon Loretta became an assistant principal in a high school
in which the principal, a woman, modeled democratic leadership:

You couldn't find a finer lady or a person who knew better
how to put a school together. That was the first time I really
had an opportunity to, for example, put a faculty handbook
together so that we had some guide as to what our school
was going to be like. The idea of people sitting together and
giving input about how our school year is going to be, it was
just wonderful. She was a very strong administrator, and she
knew where she was going to go, but she did allow input. I
think she was successful in her own way.

I also learned from another person, one of my superiors, also
an administrator. His style of administration was special because of his personality. Teachers had a lot of trust in him.
His getting along with people stood out. He would say, "If
you don't understand something, don't do, stop and ask."
Very simple.

Taking her lessons in democratic leadership from the woman, Loretta stayed on as assistant principal for 5 years and then became principal of a junior high school:

> I had never, ever, thought about being a principal. What you encounter—all the aspects of all the different personalities you work with and all the tasks that have to be performed—it's amazing! My boss was a very polished professional. He wasn't the person to say, "Okay, you've got to do it my way." He would permit me to do it in a new way, however I wanted to arrange things. He was also willing to sit down and talk about things. I learned to be tolerant.

Loretta summarized her feelings about democracy in schools, as she learned it from others:

> It's being open and giving everyone an opportunity to be part of the school. All those persons I've spoken about have actually helped to make my thinking the way it is. They all came from different walks of life. Not all of the encounters have been pleasant or positive things, but some of the negative things still help you to handle things in a different way. You reflect upon them.

> I am challenged by my relationships with adults, and I also feel I need the joy of working with youngsters. The children are so innocent and so fresh, and that is so beautiful. Then in turn I look at the adults; they are formal, yet they are just as innocent in a certain way. So it helps me to see people in different ways.

A Democratic Leader

Loretta's skill as a democratic leader seems to be founded on her interpersonal talent, her communication skills, and her ability to build trust. We talked with her at length about the primary strategies that she believes she uses to develop democracy in schools. Several factors were uppermost in her mind:

1. Give everybody a chance to have input. Loretta told us:

> It's easy for me to make a decision. It's the easiest thing, like a mother at home. You say, "Okay, this is the meal, now you're going to eat the meal that I've prepared for you." But you make for a better feeling for everybody if we talk about the meals that we are going to have this week. I don't like okra, but it's nutritious, and if we went about the selection of that particular food in a democratic way, then I might learn to like it. You might too.

2. Build a bond with people through consistent communication and acceptance:

> For a long while, when I came here, I went along with what was expected of me. The faculty agreed maybe with some of what I did, if not totally all of it. There was a tolerance until they could be sure that they could trust me. I built that trust by talking to people. I've never been a person who's been at a loss for words, never worried that I'm going to be sitting in the corner when I enter a room. I think, "Maybe I'm not a swimmer, and you might be the greatest swimmer, so we're going to find a way for us to begin talking, some kind of dialogue." And there's tolerance, if it's nothing more than my waiting for you to talk and my listening while you talk, and then you waiting to hear what I have to say. It's beginning to build a bond. We're not doing anything spectacular, nothing more than looking at one another face to face, but it helps. As a child, when I lived on Cherry Avenue, I went to the store a million times and I spoke to everybody on that street on their porches.
> "Hello, Mrs. Johnson, hello, Mrs. Davis." I mean, I spoke to everybody. I try to remember things about people, so I can later carry on a conversation. I also like to write notes to people. I even keep a *Reader's Digest* in my office for the

students. It takes just a moment for them to read it, and then they can sort of open up and calm down.

3. Communicate with the faculty. Loretta seems to be a bit of a matchmaker, connecting people and ideas:

> If there is something, some information that is worth having, everyone is going to receive it. And then I go to certain people and ask them about it. I urge them to do something about it. That's what happened with our assessment initiative; I just planted seeds. One or two people wanted to solve a problem, and now everybody's on fire with the idea.

4. Give people time. Loretta noted that sometimes she has to

> realize that maybe that person needs a little time to think about this because that person might not feel that they have anything to offer. You've just got to find ways of talking about it. Sometimes things fall on deaf ears, and you have to say, "Well, okay, that one is gone. I'll try the next one." Or maybe everybody was tired, so you put it on the back shelf, and you don't pressure people. It's just like making a cake. Maybe you don't want to try the pound cake, because that's going to take a lot of creaming the butter and getting it together. But if you're not ready to make that one, then you just use the other one, the one that you're sure of being able to make.

5. Support trial and accept failure; remember, we learn from our mistakes. Veto only when you must. Loretta noted that, in most cases, even successful task forces met with problems and went in different directions. But even if it meant that parts of the group split off, it prevented the group from just standing still. If, on occasion, she felt that disaster was imminent, she might veto something. For example, the new tardy policy instituted by the faculty was resulting in hundreds of suspensions, and Loretta felt that it was not solving problems or teaching anything, so she countermanded the rule:

I probably got a little flack on it, because they said, "Well, here, you put the rule in this handbook, and everybody knows the rule, and now you're going to change it in the middle of the stream?" I got that [negative feedback] on some of my evaluations, but I came to the group and talked about it. It went back to the liaison groups, and on some occasions we sent things back to task forces and let them study it. But I found that it's easier for me to be able to talk to you, not talk at you. I may need to say that perhaps we have not thought things through carefully.

Finally, we wanted to know the limits of shared governance in Loretta's way of thinking. She felt that she had to reserve the right to set limits on occasion, as in the case of master scheduling in which she had to refuse a teacher's first preference; on certain financial matters, although she requested input from the faculty as to how they were going to spend their money; and in dismissal cases, although other administrators would help in such matters. She does know one area that she has not become democratic in, that of personnel matters. She had included teachers in interviews for teaching candidates but only on a "very limited scale."

Advice From a Veteran

Having experienced several years of democratic, shared decision making with the faculty at Kennedy High School, Loretta was able to offer some advice to those embarking on this approach. She cautioned that faculty should not become involved in shared governance because a principal feels it is important or because it is dictated by the board or central office. According to Loretta, it needs to be something that "everybody is involved in." There should be a "concerted effort to bring everybody into it, because it will take long and hard hours." She cautioned that principals accept the plan that is developed through shared decision making and that they recognize that change does not come easily.

Loretta reminded principals of the contextuality of every school, saying, "Maybe your school is not going to function the same as another school. It is different. Each school has its different person-ality, like every child is different." She also emphasized the need for people in schools to get to substantive issues, rather than "spending all your time talking about the number of breaks that a teacher can have." Finally, she mentioned that one of her first issues on initiating shared governance was about teacher morale, liking one another, wanting to be with one another, and understanding one another. These things in particular had to come to fruition before the group was able to deal with academics.

> We had to help teachers feel good about themselves before we could decide what we were going to tackle first. Even now there are some stragglers out there, folks who are still not convinced that this is the way to do things. But you can't just wait for everybody to come into the fold. As long as you have at least 80% or 85% as a group, you go with it. They might never join forces with you, but you can't say they're not important people. I also don't believe you should keep at them until you've angered them. You have to respect their opinion, and many times, in all of this, they will see the light.

Challenges and Rewards
of Democratic Schooling

For Loretta Ford, the primary challenge of democratic schooling is developing a caring atmosphere. She cited a special volunteer program, wherein teachers go "beyond the call of duty" to become *care teachers*. Such teachers make concerted efforts to see kids and to encourage them. They provide them with special classes in English, social studies, science, and foreign language. "It's just amazing," Loretta said, "because they are growing and giving of themselves." Such personal growth and other successful elements of the Kennedy program provide her with the perks of being a democratic leader.

> People say "I'm glad I did it," or "This is a good school, and I'm gratified." Then I feel that it's because of the things that we did together that our students are doing well. It's a good

feeling; at least you're doing something good and someone else wants to hear about it usually, or maybe get involved in it. They want to talk to your teachers about how it's done. That's a high point. Now I find teachers come to me and say, "I went to this workshop. I want to share with you about this plan." I can't imagine how it would feel if no one ever wanted to do things, and you had to make them do things. If there's nothing generated from them to you or you to them, that's a very sad school.

Loretta feels that giving the types of challenges that she and her faculty and staff have given to the students at Kennedy High School is like a "dream come true." She further shared:

My whole career is like that, like a storybook. I never intended to be an administrator, it never dawned on me. My whole goal was to be the finest teacher I could be and for students in my classes to develop to their fullest potential. Each step of my development as a school teacher in the elementary school and a high school teacher and an assistant principal was necessary for me to be the best that I could be. I'd also include my being a mother of two fine sons as a highlight in my development. Also, being recognized as a leader in the democratic process has been a highlight, and I wasn't really trying to work at that. The experience I've had has been unreal.

Loretta is convinced that although it is difficult, maintaining physical and mental health has a lot to do with being a democratic leader. "It's a stressful job," she says, "but there is nothing in life that is not stressful." Getting a good night's rest and eating properly provide the necessary energy to "do your homework" and to respond with interest and enthusiasm to others:

You have to mentally think through things and let that become a part of you. You can't say to someone, "Go away, I don't have time to do this, I've got to do this other thing." You have to be willing to listen.

Having felt many times that she did not even know herself if she was right or wrong about certain decisions, Loretta admits to being cautious. She recognizes her need for constant growth and development, but she remarked:

> Once you think you're on top of all of it, that everything is going absolutely right, you might as well get ready for the fall. So I constantly go over what I'm doing and assess it to make sure I have a firm reason for what I'm doing. There are people who are going to say, "Well you don't seem to know what you are doing," so I try to keep myself girded with a lot of motivational things. I also like to be honest. And I ask parents to help me keep my perspective. They play an important role, as well as community members.

Maintaining external support has smoothed the way for Loretta. Parents of the students at Kennedy High School have always wanted to be involved in the democratic process, according to Loretta. They also let Loretta and the faculty and staff at Kennedy know if they wanted changes. Fortunately, board members have also accepted the democratic processes at Kennedy, as have the central-office members, who were delighted to have the educators involved in a shared-governance/democratic school project. Although the superintendent wanted Kennedy High School to go into a different phase of school effectiveness work, he ultimately agreed to the shared-governance efforts when the faculty and staff clearly demonstrated their support and interest in it. The chamber of commerce has even supported these efforts, and a representative from the Boeing Company went with the faculty and staff on a retreat and trained them in team building.

What is the future of democracy at Kennedy High School? Loretta believes that the staff should be asked every year whether they wish to continue operating under democratic principles.

> The principal and the strong leaders of the school need to be alike in their thinking in order to work together. That is one force that always has to be in place. You also have to have a group of teachers who are willing to be involved and to work hard to make things happen. They can be hired, and

you can have a dialogue with candidates about this. It's important, because there are some people who would really not be happy under these conditions.

Also, Loretta stressed that

the dignity, the worth of a person, the importance of fair play, the importance of learning, the importance of talking about people's talents in such a way as to give them confidence are crucial. It can be difficult in the face of economic conditions such as those at Kennedy or in the face of instability, crime, and drugs, or simply because students don't have that self-esteem. I guess any of the ills that are associated with these social conditions make it hard to be successful. That's why there's a place for shared governance. There are also constraints from state standards or local standards. Shared governance provides an opportunity for everyone to be creative, to suggest different ways of obtaining our goals.

Final Words

Predictably, when asked about her philosophy, Loretta once again spoke of the idea of family and the primacy of working with students:

I want our school to be a place where people are eager to come to work and eager to work with youngsters, with their problems even. Such a school is one in which people are eager to work with parents, eager to listen and come up with solutions. That is shared governance, that is democratic, and we are working toward it at Kennedy. We don't think we're perfect by a long shot, but we're working at making our students the focal point. Everyone is sincere, and the work in our liaison groups is the finest that we have ever done. We've gotten to know one another, and we're finding more reasons to celebrate. We have a family concept, and when we have a problem it's no longer just my problem, it's everybody's problem. Even our relationship with the central office has changed. They are very proud of us. We are often asked to share with other schools and other settings in our community what we are doing.

Discussion Questions

1. To what degree and in what ways did Loretta's early experiences (personal and professional) influence her approach to leadership?
2. Do you agree with Loretta's position regarding her power of veto?
3. From what you know, does Loretta exhibit strength in initiating democratic structures/processes and in the five primary strategies she professes to develop?
4. Do you think that morale is often a critical issue when initiating shared-governance/democratic schooling?
5. What other things might Loretta do to expand the democratic approach to schooling at Kennedy High School?
6. How would you characterize Loretta's stage of development as a democratic leader?

6

Guardian of the Mission
The Suburban
High School Experience

I'm not terribly threatened by somebody who knows more than I do, but I think a lot of people in my position are. They get into the position of principal or assistant principal for different reasons. Maybe it has more to do with their insecurity or their zeal for power than with the betterment of kids and teachers.

—Tim Casey, Principal
Newton County High School

Twenty years ago Tim Casey, who is white, was teaching at a large Catholic high school on Long Island. A physical education and biology major, Tim had previously taught at both the elementary and middle school levels. He was also an active element in the formation of a faculty council at the school, a body that was "basically designed to advise and assist the principal as well as the entire administrative team with curricular, instructional, and management issues." Although the impetus for formation of the faculty council may have been ongoing conflict, Tim credits the principal with having a good idea:

The principal was a rather progressive person. He had a doctorate in education and a very interesting philosophy. There were two camps in the school; one was very, very rigid, and the other, like him, wanted to provide kids opportunities to be responsible. There were also a lot of loosey-goosey types whose attitudes with kids were "different," and the principal came down hard on those particular people. He ended up firing five. So there was a constant clash. I don't know whether the conflict created the idea of the faculty council. . . . I tend to think the principal created the idea. The first year it never happened, but the second year I became part of the leadership group, and we really tried to deal with healing and bringing these factions together.

Tim felt that he began to change after the firings.

It forced me to broaden my horizons, to look at things in a different way. I argued with this principal, or discussed; we really didn't argue. I shared my views about the terminations, and I guess I began to grow. I didn't look at things as critically. I used to believe that if a school had all the same type of people, it would be a great place, but it's not. We need to celebrate diversity. I look to hire people who are different—in all respects—rather than people who are alike. For students, you need to bring in other perspectives that a typical student will not see. If you don't have different points of view, you don't progress; you go backward.

In time, Tim discovered that he was "much more tolerant" of different points of view than he used to be. His new philosophy was to "bring out the best in each person" because then he or she "will excel." He realized that was the foundation of the concept of shared governance, that

somebody else's opinion isn't necessarily wrong because it's different from mine. It's a fact that a collective decision is better than an individual decision. And a collective decision without manipulation is important.

Tim volunteered his time for the shared-governance effort. He became chairman of the council for 2 years, after which he left the school to complete a master's degree in school administration. Thus Tim's first experience with "participative management" or "collective/ shared decision making," as he variously calls it, was focused on far more than "administrivia," and it triggered a revolution in his thinking about shared decision making among educators.

In subsequent visits to a neighboring school district, Tim observed in action a similarly designed, all-district council, consisting of school representatives, parents, and students. Each member of the council, including the district superintendent, had only one vote on decisions. Tim credits the superintendent, a man he "admired for having such courage," with providing a working model for Tim of collective decision making. Shortly thereafter, Tim himself became a principal (albeit reluctantly, because "where the teacher meets the kid is where the rubber hits the road"), and through the department chairpersons he was able to initiate democratic structures. He remembered:

> I had only one vote, and we began with the very simple issues. You know, "Where is somebody going to park?" Then we moved into the instructional and curriculum issues. The northeastern part of the country, where I was, was faced with severely declining enrollments, and we were constantly being faced with teachers being "excessed" [let go]. So we created some unique and interesting things that were curricular and instructional in nature, and at the same time we were able to maintain morale and keep jobs. We also really developed a vision of where our school was going. When I left, the hiring of the new principal was a democratic hiring; they had a teacher and a union representative on the committee and the entire discussion was about democratic leadership. The new superintendent emphasized to people that "this is what we're trying to do."

Learning From Experience:
Initiating Shared Governance

Tim again attended graduate school in another state and, true to his instructional bent, earned a doctorate in curriculum and supervision. He also took a position as an assistant principal of a large suburban high school, in which he and the principal initiated shared-governance processes and principles. His highly successful experience in those attempts further prepared Tim to do the same at a brand new model county high school, in which he has recently been appointed principal. We asked Tim to talk about the business of initiating democratic governance, or shared decision making, in schools previously void of such approaches:

> How does one initiate or institutionalize shared governance? I've thought about that and discussed it with others. Four things: First of all, I think there has to be a readiness. The faculty has to be ready and the principal has to be ready, because once you give up power, you can't take it back. It's not one of those things you can have both ways. Time is also a very important factor. You have to have people who are willing to donate a tremendous amount of time. In my role as assistant principal or principal, I know I'm going to work 50, 60, 70 hours a week, and teachers aren't used to that, but they've got to be willing to donate time. The third and fourth pieces are that it's got to become part of the culture, and it's got to become policy, not only in the school, but in the district.

> The case in any school that's moving toward an empowerment movement is that you're moving from an autocratic situation to a democratic situation. It's incumbent on the principal that we not manipulate the situation, that we bend over backward to have a real democratic situation with honest input. And we need to establish a partnership. The teacher can't be accountable for everything, the kid can't be accountable for everything, and the parent can't be accountable for everything. It has to be mutual.

Comparing his experience in the northeastern school with his belief that the four elements of readiness, time, culture, and policy are essential to shared-governance efforts, Tim explained that the program may have been somewhat instructive about initiating shared governance but that it faltered after Tim's departure, apparently because relevant policy, which might have helped to ensure continued shared governance, had not been enacted.

> We did some of that in the northeast; the department chairmen, the teachers, all of us together built the culture, but we didn't have a policy. Although the superintendent hired a person (to fill the position I left) who articulated that he was going to be a shared-governance-type leader, he never did any of that. Teachers there now say, "We used to have this power, and now we don't have it. It's important that the curriculum have a unified focus, but we don't do that anymore because it's not important to him." So the whole emphasis changed because they don't have a policy.

This, too, was instructive for Tim because his next position, the assistant principalship in a suburban high school, was marked by his own more systematic efforts to operate the school by shared governance. However, and predictably, having a policy did not compensate for a lack of culture, time, and readiness:

> I was hired at Dayton High School because Jack, the principal, wanted to put in shared governance. Unlike what a lot of people think, you can't just go to a workshop and then institute shared governance. It takes all those things we mentioned. I was cognizant of that, and so we wrote the by-laws of how it works, checks and balances, a policy of sorts. It's taking time to develop the culture, though, 3 years to get to the point where people believe it's going to work. It used to be that people would come to the meetings when there was a critical situation. But Dayton High School is now getting to the point where the culture is catching up with the policy. Time and the readiness of the principal is still a problem at times, though, because he is not yet ready to relinquish all the power you need to relinquish to make it work.

I'll say this, having been a principal, then assistant principal, and seeing it from the inside and the outside as both a school person and as a university person [liaison to shared-governance programs], I believe the following: The principal who is able to effectively initiate a shared-governance policy has significantly more power than the one who does not. You might not have power to dictate anymore, but you have power to succeed. It's very interesting, and I've seen it several times in my own experiences.

Starting Fresh

As Tim begins work this year at the shiny new county high school of 1,100 students, he is clear that he wants to "share the power" and establish trust with faculty and staff members. Given the chance to start fresh, tabula rasa, and given the advantage of his experiences with shared governance, he is clearly determined and confident that he can institute a shared-governance approach. "I've already taken some steps and solicited opinions," he reported. "The chairmen have been involved in the process of hiring teachers. Not a big thing, but it was a joint decision." We asked him to elaborate on this decision and others that involve teachers. With his rolled-up sleeves and loosened tie, this distinctively northeastern, genial, and highly verbal school leader shared the following:

It was something that needed to be done. First of all, I'm not going to pretend to know enough about math, science, English, or social studies to hire all of these people. I'm also not the one working directly with them. It's important for me to get the other teachers' opinions, so I did that. I've also invited two department chairmen to sit in on the selection process of the assistant principal. The other thing I've done is to create the master schedule in such a way that chairmen are all off at the same time; they have an additional planning period, and we are all going to meet once a week or once a month or whatever is necessary to begin to plan together.

What I want to do is begin to establish trust. I think trust is
what you get from people when you tell them the truth; you
can't lie to people, and you can't double-cross people. I also
want to establish the fact that their opinions count. It's going
to be interesting to see how different people react, especially
since the former principal was exactly the opposite.

Tim also spoke of the satisfactions and gratifications that come
from sharing the governance of a school:

As a result of allowing others to take a leadership role, you
have more influence. You have more power, so successes are
magnified. There's also a lot of satisfaction in that you can
take pride in your school—the old things, the new things,
the history, the achievements of the kids. It's much like
teaching . . . there's a lot of rewards.

Tim's Code: A System of Beliefs

As our interviews with Tim progressed and as we visited him
during his assistant principalship and recently at the inception of
his new principalship, we began to get a clearer picture of Tim's core
beliefs, those things that drive his professional actions. Over the
course of time, Tim's experiences and the deep discussions he has
had with educators, researchers, and friends have led him to several
conclusions. For example, Tim has a strong belief that the classroom
is the center of action, and this defines his role, as well as the role of
the teacher:

The whole structure [of education] is upside down. The kid
ought to be at the top, and the teacher next, and then the department chairman, and then the superintendent at the
bottom. I don't even think I'm good enough to teach anymore, although I thought I was a fairly effective teacher. It's
a hard, hard job, much harder than the job I have. I think as an
administrator you help facilitate change and facilitate their
instruction and facilitate a lot of things. But you can't make

"it" happen, and you don't affect the kids unless you affect the teachers. Teaching—that's the really important role.

Given his belief in the classroom as the center of action, Tim emphasizes listening to teachers and enabling them to pursue ideas:

> Who can better direct what needs to be facilitated than the people who are in the classrooms? It's easier, quicker, and cleaner for one person or two people [principals] to dictate what happens in a school. But it's not better. If you listen to the teachers, that's a democratic process. You have the opportunity to listen. If the decisions are made not necessarily through compromise, but through deliberation and dialogue, then it's going to make more sense to the people who are in the center of the interaction. Why, how would you do it any other way?

> I believe that the kids need to demonstrate their learning through publications and other achievements. I believe in the science fair, the student yearbook, the student newspaper, the literary magazine, the parent publication done by students. They experience then what happens in the world: frustrations, debating what you believe in, reporting honestly, understanding restrictions, expressing opinions. I believe in what we did at Dayton High School when we created a ninth-grade support team; we got a grant, and they put a million bucks into it countywide. The principal had given us room to do it.

Indeed, Tim is succinct, direct, and bold to the point of terseness regarding the fundamentals of shared-governance operations. His beliefs form a sort of code of democracy for him and guide his actions daily:

> The principles I believe in are the same principles that this country is founded on. It sometimes makes it tough, sometimes makes it very, very difficult because of the additional time it takes. I have to talk and listen and provide

opportunities for people to get what they need. And the only way they can get what they need is if they have a voice. I believe that all people have worth, that everybody's opinion is important, that no one person knows all, and that the leadership position is a support role.

Drawing on his time as a graduate student as well as his experiences in the schools, Tim also developed an anti-isolationist approach:

During my master's program, I was able to look back on what I did as a practitioner and evaluate what I did, whether it was good, bad, or indifferent. When I was in my doctoral program, I was able to reflect and to maintain a professional dialogue with others. The dialogue is what is typically missing in the teaching and administrative environment. We're all isolated.

The new school I am in has largely been built to facilitate professional dialogue, although there are still a few building barriers between people. In some cases the teachers chose not to have individual desks in the classrooms. There are teacher workrooms with desks, closets, and file cabinets, and these faculty rooms are not places where teachers come together to gripe, but they come to gather and talk about their profession. On the negative side, they are too sharply focused [by department], but we are going to do some things to facilitate cross-department dialogue. We've got to provide time for it; IBM gives people that time, General Motors gives them that time, so why don't we give them that time?

Working With
Other Constituencies

Such beliefs are bolstered by Tim's strong stance when it comes to working—in a straightforward manner—with central-office staff members and the superintendent:

Sometimes my relationship with my supervisor was hostile because I would say, "I'm sorry. I can't do that. Find someone else to do that." I guess I was insubordinate, but even when we had the same values, we didn't always have the same beliefs. Conflict and confrontation are easier to live with than telling white lies to get out of a situation. Part of the reason that I wanted this new position was that I felt that there was not only support from the central office and the superintendent, but there was a basic ethical understanding which put me on firm ground. If you don't consider yourself a political animal, you become one in the principal's position. How do you walk that line among ethics, values, your belief system, and political expediency?

Indeed, Tim also spoke of the difficulty of developing an understanding of democratic schooling between parents and community leaders with whom he strives daily to establish a partnership:

It's hard to get this across to the community. You have to do it through your written material, your vision, the way you articulate things to kids. You use the right terminology when you talk with parents, and you hope you have a common language and develop a shared understanding. It's very hard, and it takes a long time. We also need the business people. They send money and want to be part of the decision process; that's when you've developed ownership, which is different from buy-in. Buy-in is when we tell people what we're going to do and they like it, but ownership is when they create, which has a long-term effect.

Letting Go

Who is this man who is willing to step forward against control, bureaucracy, isolationism, and the loneliness of the one-room schoolhouse? Clearly, his ideas pushed against the edges of the typical educational enterprise in his last two positions. He reported seeing

teachers early in his career who were "stifled," and he told us that
the shared-governance approach "just made sense" to him. But what
about his personality, his character? What makes one ready, we
asked him, to share the governance of a school? Several of Tim's
comments are revealing:

> I try to seek out things that will make the school better, to
> support those teachers, to facilitate the program, to go above
> and beyond the call of duty. As a principal, I have the
> power and authority to establish a curriculum, for example.
> And I can probably get a good committee together. I can ask
> people to join, and I can create meetings, and we can get some
> things done. I have power and I have authority, but I also
> have the responsibility to create success for our school.

> If a group of teachers forms a curriculum committee, many
> of the same things will happen, but the success and the pro-
> ductivity of the committee will be significantly more. This
> is a result of being democratic and allowing the people to
> set the direction. This, as opposed to manipulating how they
> set the direction, allows a trust factor to develop which gives
> you unbelievable power, I think. By allowing others to take
> the leadership role, you have more influence as a leader.
> You're much more powerful.

> You've got to focus on the process. It's ongoing. It's contin-
> ual. You find yourself reeducating people that things take
> time, that we have a process. The layman, or parent, or super-
> intendent may have a lack of understanding about things
> that would usually be a simple, quick, efficient decision, but
> now are not. But the benefits of taking time may be with the
> group development and group dynamics more than with
> the actual decision.

> You've got to let go. I remember our principal at Dayton; I
> could usually talk with him as easily as I talked with teach-
> ers. He would come to me and say he didn't like what was
> going on, and I might say, "You've got to let it happen because

you've chosen this as the way." A lot of times, though, I bit my tongue.

We asked Tim if he used the power of veto in his own work with teachers. "Absolutely none, absolutely none," he asserted vehemently. So we asked what he would do if he saw that things were headed for disaster. "Let them fall on their face," came his immediate reply, and then, more thoughtfully, "That's a learning process. Very seldom would people fall flat on their face. Remember, the people who make decisions want it to work, and they do what they need to make it work." What about the fine line between embracing diverse opinions and committing to the same philosophy, mission, or goals, we wanted to know. "The commitment is to the kids," Tim declared. And finally, "That's what our democratic process is, a balance of philosophies, opinions, and differences. The commitment to excellence, to instruction, or to kids is not unique to any one philosophy."

Tim also resists artificial limitations. He recalls a turf battle at Dayton High School in which the shared-governance executive committee members were offended at not having been included in budget decisions, which were still decided by the department chairpersons. Although he recognizes the need to have resolved role issues between the two bodies at Dayton, he now feels that "there are very few things that cannot be decided by the group, particularly in terms of operations, procedures, curriculum, and instruction." According to Tim, the last bastion of administrative decision making is dismissal of weak teachers, for the protection of the faculty as well as the individual teacher involved.

Reflections on the Past and Future

As he embarks on his new principalship, Tim anticipates stresses similar to those of the past:

There are things that are stressful because of the position, whether you're democratic or you're not. Time is a major stress. You can't start a task, research a task, and complete a task. I've got stuff all over the place, and I spend too much wasted time fumbling for stuff. Right now, we don't have procedures for crises in place—evacuations, bomb scares, riots. It's a priority. And many procedures have to be developed through democratic-type operations.

I think you deal with a group. Don't deal with individuals. Sometimes in talking to an individual if you express an opinion, the person then becomes your ally in the group situation, and you find yourself playing off this person, or the person is playing off of you. Before you know it, you have, in fact, manipulated the group even though it was not your intent. So you deal with issues with the group.

Tim is also wary of the pitfalls awaiting him in the new position and cites his personal weaknesses: giving little attention to classroom observation, failing to record for others the experiences of his school, and failing to complete efforts at evaluation of programs:

We all know that supervision of instruction makes a difference. But we all attend to discipline and attendance, for example, because it's there every day, because it's knocking on our door all the time. And no, we don't have that many people knocking on our door saying, "Please come supervise me."

The writing about and evaluation of our projects, whether it be a narrow focus, as in a special project on the ninth grade, or a broader focus in terms of the whole school, . . . if we don't put it down on paper and evaluate it, we can't improve on it. And then it becomes another one of those pilot projects that just goes away. I don't discipline myself enough to sit down and complete the writing and evaluation part, which goes back to action research—which is probably the critical component of shared governance. It's the hardest thing to maintain. We think we know. But when you look at the numbers and the records (and we really do quantitative and qualitative data gathering), we really didn't know.

You've got to be willing to give people not only your time, but your attention. It's sometimes difficult, like when you're sitting in an interview, and you need to go on to the next thing.

The higher you are on the chart, the less you need to say. I usually sit in these meetings, and I try to listen. I write myself little notes to listen because every time you speak, people look at you—it's the E. F. Hutton thing. When the principal says something, it carries significantly more weight than anybody else. It may not have any value or merit. It may be just a thought that comes and goes. In the dynamic of a group, the person with the most authority and responsibility should take less and less of the active participation.

Tim is also aware of shouldering significant and important responsibilities, those of being the "guardian of the mission" and supporter of teachers taking risks and teachers learning:

The school needs to create a mission and a vision. As leader, I have to be the guardian of the mission. I have to be the champion of the mission. The school district is in the process of doing it from a district point of view, and the school has to do it from a school point of view. And I've got to sit down and remind people that these are the guidelines and that if something doesn't fit into the mission and our vision, then it's not something we ought to be doing. That becomes the yardstick by which we measure the decisions we make. The ultimate decision is in the best interest of kids.

Yes, there needs to be a sense of urgency about subject matter and about teaching kids, but we lose sight of the fact that there are more things in this world than 50 minutes of history. Learning takes many different avenues. And it's also about teachers. I guess I could use Barth's discussion of a "community of learners," the thought that it's okay to learn, it's okay to go back to school, it's not only okay but it's desirable. It's something we'll support, even if we have to sweat financially.

When you free people to take a chance, some extraordinary things happen. People work much harder for that success because it's their idea and it's something they want to do. Amazing things happen in the classroom, amazing things happen with kids, and they kind of explode under that kind of leadership from teachers. Teachers become better leaders, too. They're willing to take the ball and run with it, so to speak, if they know they're not going to get their hands slapped for doing it. I have seen teachers who were reluctant to take any kind of stand in the past come in and say, "Hey, I want to get involved in this issue." They're willing to take a risk, and they're not afraid to share what they're doing with other people. They're not afraid to talk, and once they begin talking, instruction gets better.

We asked Tim about his views on the future of democratic schooling. Tim referred to the basic restructuring that he feels must take place before significant movement toward democratic forms of schooling occurs:

The kids are isolated from what happens out there in the real world. We need to expand, to make our educational system more a part of the community and more part of the real world. Also, outcome-based education has a lot of hope, but it really hasn't dealt with assessment, and we can't bring it in yet because we haven't changed the [basic] structure. I'm sorry to say it, but the educational foot does not fit the factory shoe, and yet we continue to put education into the factory model. It doesn't fit.

Before we parted, Tim marveled that we were doing a case study of his career. Relaxing in his attractive, well-appointed new office with adjoining conference room, he mused about whether his case will be interesting to anybody else. He wondered if his work in the "jewel" of the county will be different. And then, in his characteristically determined and purposeful way, he said,

Well, I've got this new experience ahead of me. I'd like to write and write about it and evaluate it. I'd like to start a case study on it . . . you know what I mean.

Discussion Questions

1. How can a principal, who is new to a school, establish trust, relinquish power, and smooth the transition from the former principal?

2. In what areas and to what degree should teachers be involved in schoolwide decisions? Under what conditions should there be limitations to such involvement?

3. When Tim speaks of "allowing" teachers to lead, is he consistent with his avowed philosophy of shared governance?

4. Is there a difference between a democratic philosophy and a democratic process? Should an implemented process survive a change in leadership?

5. Compare how Tim's faculty uses action research with that of your own faculty (and as you read on, that of Tommy Johnson's faculty in Chapter 7). What causes the differences between the two?

7

Gentle Pushes

Strength and Humanism
in a Rural Secondary School

*After 4 years, we have evolved now to more of an atmosphere of
trust than there was at first. But at that time, they weren't ready
to give input and I wasn't ready to wait for them, so I went ahead
and did some things.*

—Tommy Johnson, Principal
Belmont County Secondary School

Tommy Johnson, 46 years old and white, is big, friendly, and joyful.
His handshake is strong, and his engaging smile makes you feel
instantly comfortable. He gives the impression of confidence, energy, sensitivity, and a warm heart. Dressed casually and moving
with the ease of a trim former athlete, Tommy acknowledges every
person by name who passes him as he moves through the halls of
rural Belmont County Secondary School. In turn, he is always addressed as Mr. Johnson, in the customarily respectful manner of
address for this rural part of the South. Tommy's dry humor and
heavily accented speech is peppered with expressions found only in
the South: They didn't have a "big ol' tax base"; They were supposed
to do that "from the get-go"; They could use a little more "hep"; and

"Dang it, we're going to do it anyway." As we talk, it is clear from Tommy's demeanor and words that he is in the right place, he loves his work, and he is an active advocate for children:

> My goal is to challenge each one of the students and prepare them for what they will be doing later.

> In hiring teachers, we want a flexible teacher coming on board who will listen and who will do what's best for the kids. We have a good mix now; we have the "young lions" and also the veterans, experienced teachers who are not set in their ways. We're looking for stability, hiring teachers who either graduated from a real small school or who have lived in a small town and who will become a part of the community. We don't want a merry-go-round, with different people every year, or people who are scared of a small town.

> The things we want to tackle are the things that are going to benefit the kids, in the end.

It was not in Tommy's plan to become a school administrator, although one might have predicted it from his life experiences: He was elected a councilman at Boy's State, was captain of his high school football team, entered Reserve Officers Training Corps (ROTC), served in the military, and on becoming a physical education teacher also became a coach. Asked if he can point to an experience that prompted him to become a democratic educational leader, Tommy initially alludes to his sense of equal and shared responsibility:

> I can't point to one amazing revelation. It was just something in the way I was brought up. I always felt like I would rather lead by example than get up there and give lectures or whatever. We administrators are at the FFA [Future Farmers of America] banquet, the FHA [Future Homemakers of America] banquet, the ball games, the literary club meetings, and we even drive the bus every now and then; the people feel like, "He's not asking me to do something that he hasn't ever done." I just feel like I can't ask somebody to dig a foxhole if I haven't dug a foxhole myself.

Indeed, Tommy is the first to "dig a foxhole":

> I can't ask them to go write a curriculum guide if I haven't been there myself. And I try to go to as much of the staff development as I can. I also get in those classrooms to find out what they're doing and to support them as much as I can.

The Formative Years

Musing about his youth, Tommy noticed a spark for his emergent leadership style in his home life:

> I was brought up in a Christian home with values, and there were fair expectations of me. I also always had somebody there supporting me, and I knew that they were interested in what I was doing. So I think if you are going to be selected to be the, quote, leader of a bunch of people, then you've got to know what's important to those people and support them as much as you can when they're doing what you ask them to do. I've been brought up to have respect and empathy for somebody's input; everybody might not think the same way about something, and you need to be fair.

In addition, Tommy's leadership talent may be a reflection of the style of his own head coach, who provided Tommy with an early model of what was to become Tommy's approach:

> He would pull me in and ask me, "What do y'all think about this?" I always appreciated that; I felt like I was representing my teammates when I told him what I thought would work or not.

After teaching and coaching for 10 years, Tommy left education for 1 year. He had become disillusioned with his (and other teachers') lack of input. The negative feelings from his teaching experience stayed with him and formed the basis of his approach to working with teachers.

As a teacher, I had some ideas, some of which were listened to and some not. It was frustrating, you know, not to be heard and frustrating not to know what's going on. I think from that I got two principles which I hold to: You need to communicate with people and let them know what's going on, and you need to at least listen to them. You know they feel more involved in the whole process if they have some input and communication.

Within a year of reentering teaching, Tommy became a middle school assistant principal. He reported to us that the principal he worked under also helped mold his leadership style. Tommy had served on the school's leadership team, and he took note of what he thought, at the time, was an open and democratic leadership style on the part of the principal. In retrospect (and in light of Tommy's own evolving democratic style), Tommy doubts whether that principal was perceived by the faculty to be truly democratic.

Getting Started at Belmont

Today, Tommy is in his fourth year as principal of a combined middle and high school of 800 students, half of whom are on the free- or reduced-lunch program. It is his own hometown to which he has returned. Deeply rural, the county of 8,000 people is proud of its secondary school, which is nestled in a town of 2,500. The school's racial mix is evenly split between African American and white students of middle-socioeconomic status, and the school buildings are neat and clean, though modestly appointed. Emphasis throughout the buildings is on school colors and events, trophies, and student recognition.

Predictably, Tommy is reluctant to take credit for his school's advances in democratic governance. He notes that as early as 5 years ago the school was headed toward site-based management by virtue of the faculty's considerable input to staff development plans; edicts to implement certain programs were never issued from the central office. Yet, on his arrival 3 years ago, Tommy soon saw the faculty's hue and cry for more involvement:

When I came in that first year, I read the staff development
needs assessment. There was a common theme that came
through in comments like "I don't know what's going on,"
"Somebody needs to communicate with me more," and "I
feel like I never know 'til after the fact what happened." So
the relationship I built was to get an opinion from everybody.
In the democratic situation you can listen to a lot of people,
let them sound off, let them come in and sit down and cry
or fuss or whatever. But you just listen to what they've got
to say, and you be concerned.

At the same time, Tommy has been known to listen selectively, as he
himself reported:

The opinion you really take to heart is your business. The ones
you listen to are the ones that matter, the well-respected teachers, the ones with the good relationship with the students,
those who get along well with the other faculty members.
Not the ones who are out there on their own.

Initiating democratic structures was not particularly easy for
Tommy and the faculty. Tommy was warned by board members that
he "better not listen to all that those teachers say and do everything
that they want you to do, because they'll get you in trouble." Although
Tommy notes that "the parents in this community pretty much trust
that we know what we're doing (we have a corps of residents who
attended this school themselves, and so did their children, and their
children's children)," Tommy feels "lucky" that decisions made by
the 35 professional faculty members haven't "come back to haunt"
them. He also feels the press of state regulations, which inhibit
efforts such as building in an extra class period in the day or
changing the local graduation requirements, which are currently
heavy with vocational-technical curricula. Yet Tommy faces these
and other barriers to democratic functioning with courage:

A big drawback in this whole process is the time it takes to
throw something to the faculty, get their input, come back

again, find out what they said, then make your decision. You can spend all your time getting input and then not be able to run the school every day. I think the more complicated the process is, the less effective the initiative is, so you keep it simple. We are small, and that's an advantage; our leadership team members can poll the people in their liaison groups in 2 hours or half a school day. I think the time you spend communicating on the front end saves you a lot of headaches on the tail end when it comes to trying to implement some of this stuff. It's not so hard to get them fired up about something we really need to talk about, but nobody likes to change. And teachers have been in their little classrooms, some of them teaching the same old way for umpteen years.

In their fourth year of operating as a democratic school, Belmont County Secondary School's "tight-knit family" of teachers (as Tommy affectionately calls it) has a rotating leadership team that consists of representatives elected from department areas, many of whom are not the appointed chairpersons. This team meets for 2 days during the summer, when the members study the school's action research results and data, hold lengthy discussions, decide on goals, and draft annual plans. The leadership team has a special kind of honor, as Tommy relates:

> They all see that through our work together nobody is trying to pull any wool over anybody's eyes; we just want to do what's best for kids. So we get a new person rotating into the representative position, and it mellows out attitudes sometimes. We also look to see who has never been to a League [of Professional Schools] meeting, and we'll send two rookies every time. It shows everybody that, hey, we're just trying to find out what everybody's doing that's best for their kids. If it fits our situation and we think it would be good for us, we may look at doing it. It's developing now so that we don't have some people who you feel are out in left field or opinions that aren't the majority. But you're always going to have two or three of those.

A review of Belmont County Secondary School's annual reports, prepared by facilitators from the statewide shared-governance group, the League of Professional Schools, reveals an interesting pattern in this school's efforts to restructure and to embrace democratic governance over the past 3 years. Initially, the focus was on giving teachers "voice" and handling technical or operational concerns (e.g., parking, lunch arrangements). Soon, teachers began to talk about and make changes regarding educational matters, such as grade reporting and pretesting. As the teachers' sense of involvement grew, so did the involvement of parents and, to some degree, students. Faculty members then began to talk about goals, to plan together, and to conduct action research related to instructional issues and decisions they had to make. Most recently, the focus has been on curriculum integration, a major, schoolwide effort. Tommy described the development of this focus:

> It started off as, "How can we help our at-risk kids?" The countywide leadership team came in for 2 days of staff development, and we looked at the action research. The most at-risk kids at our school are the ninth graders. The failure rate is high, the dropout rate is high, and more of them go into special programs than at any other grade. We arranged for ninth-grade teachers . . . to meet together once or twice a month to discuss the kids and see if there's a common thing they can do to help the kids. That was the seed that was planted for curriculum integration: It started off kid centered, and it evolved into general academics because of the failure rate. The consensus is that our teaching is too fragmented. If you solve a problem in the real world, you've got to use math, science, English, and social studies. It's also the middle school concept.

Tommy's Strategies
for Democratic Governance

We asked Tommy to talk about the strategies he has used to implement democratic governance at Belmont County Secondary School.

At first he struggled, saying, "I never have thought about it. I don't think I've ever been able to class myself as one type of leader, the benevolent autocrat or whatever, because I think you've got to be each of the types at some point in time." With more thought, however, he was able to elaborate on several keys to the democratic approach, as he saw it. The following are Tommy's strategies for democratic governance.

Simplify meetings. "This is the tool I employ," Tommy said. "No teacher who I know loves to sit in a meeting and listen to somebody go on and on about something that's not pertinent to what they're doing." Tommy runs an organized meeting. To that end, he screens out "superfluous or useless" discussions that consume valuable time that teachers might otherwise use to deal with instructional concerns. "I think that the more complicated the process is, the less effective the whole initiative is," he said.

For faculty meetings, no agenda is built, and the faculty have decided to meet once a week "so we won't have a big old long agenda." Tommy notes, "We try to do our homework through a task force or study committee before a presentation is made to the faculty." It took the group 2 years to put together some by-laws to guide their efforts; during this time, "we knew we were flying by the seat of our pants, but that was fine with everybody because everybody trusted each other." Minutes are "very sketchy" and not published but read back at the next meeting. Items may be brought up by anyone on the leadership team, and votes seldom need to be taken, because the group tries to work by consensus. To describe the group's history of decision making by consensus, Tommy told the following story:

> We've only had three occasions where the teachers had to come down and actually vote on something. We were split on the senior exam exemption issue, as well as on the requirements for valedictorian and salutatorian. There were several different ideas expressed on those, so we put it out for a vote. We haven't had a bunch of controversial issues that we have been split on, and we've pretty much been able to get consensus.

Tommy expects that the current major effort to integrate the curriculum may bring some disagreements to the fore and may push the faculty to a more intense level of talk. This, he feels, will be a true test of their trust in and development of problem-solving skills. Still, he hearkens to a decision about grouping students when he says, "We knew we had some doubters, but [with democratic governance] we have a built-in sounding board for input, plus we made a research-based decision, a sound decision with input."

Do the "front end" work. "One of the worst things we get in education is surprises, and nobody likes a surprise," Tommy offered. "I just think that everybody ought to know the wavelength you're on." In this vein, Tommy is inclined to an intense communication style. He shares anticipated changes well before an official memo or word comes from the central office. He actively links teachers' opinions or thoughts and central-office administrators' thinking. He lets people know that a change may or may not occur but that the current thinking is along certain lines. He avoids big shocks and shares his own ruminations about impending decisions. He may, for example, ask a teacher what he or she thinks about teaching a different class or advising a club long before the need emerges to find a replacement. "Don't wait 3 more weeks until the big memo arrives saying it is a fact," he advises. "Let them know at the front end." His experience with building a large addition to the school demonstrates this:

> When we started the building program, there were all sorts of rumors, like so-and-so is going to have to leave his room, and there's going to be some different thing in that room, or whatever. Well, every time the superintendent would tell me something, or every time I'd sit down with the architect, or every time our committee would go visit a media center, or every time the assistant superintendent would go look at a technology lab, I'd tell the leadership team about it. This is a small community, and we've had as many rumors as anywhere. So I take a lot of time, I do a lot of writing of little memos. As soon as I get off the phone to somebody about these things, I go tell them what I know.

Stay tuned in, but bypass resisters. Although Tommy's leadership style is one of "communicate, communicate, and then communicate again," he still feels the need to check signals with teachers that he trusts implicitly. He gathers input from teacher-leaders; still, as much as he works at being open, he admits that he may not always have complete information, and he recognizes that some teachers may remain on the opposite side of certain issues. At one point in our interviews, he told us that he feels assured that he is perceived as democratic because, "I just kind of get vibes," but he also later confided that he values the "other set of eyes" found in feedback from select teachers:

> I've got certain people on the faculty who will sit down and level with me, and they won't say what I want to hear. I mean, they'll tell me straight out. To do this, you've got to pick the people who are the most in tune with what's going on. It's not that you have "pets" or that you show any favoritism, but you know, every faculty has two or three people who are—how do I want to say this?—who are not as democratically oriented or not as group oriented as the other teachers. And certain ones have a vision or a goal of where they want to be 5 years from now, and you get opinions from them, the ones who represent what the majority of the teachers think.

> When we first went into democratic governance, we said, "If you folks don't want to buy into this, that's fine. But just don't keep the rest of us from doing something a little different or making a change." In some of the initiatives we have now, we're seeing what Carl Glickman says: You've got to get the one-room schoolhouses out of the school. So many teachers for so long have wanted to go into their room and close the door, saying, "This is my domain. I don't care what anybody else is doing now, just leave me alone, and I don't want to try all those other things." Those people are a constraint to democratic governance. Well, we're trying to turn this into "our" school, not "my" classroom. We've got to try to educate the folks as to what the alternatives to the one-room schoolhouse are and why those are better than just

putting up walls around what you are doing. Also, when you have shared decision making and you hit on something that works, there's a lot greater sense of accomplishment than there was when you were told you had to do it.

Support experimentation. Sprinkled throughout Tommy's lengthy, excited talk about fledgling instructional programs was evidence of support for innovation, experimentation, and professional planning. For example, he told us:

We're so small that we can't take an 11th-grade English teacher and an 11th-grade history teacher out of class during the same period, because that leaves you with 60 kids you cannot schedule anywhere during that period. So we're going to use a little staff development money to give them a common planning time once a month. That is a shared decision, and we're going to make it work. Also, every teacher up here goes to at least one or two conferences a year, either with the professional organization or on a particular topic of interest.

I think you get so excited about what you're doing that—I don't want to say you ignore the resisters, but—you go ahead and accent the positive and don't worry about the negative. If you get enough positive, the negatives are going to finally jump on the ship. They may not be the most gung ho people in the world, but they're going to show up just because everybody else was so fired up about what they were doing.

Initiate democratic governance only with the support of the faculty. Although Tommy was highly motivated to initiate democratic-governance efforts at Belmont County High School, he wisely stepped back as faculty members made their own decisions about joining the League of Professional Schools and embarking on such a project. In fact, it was the high school, not the middle school, that joined initially. In this case, timing was of the utmost importance.

When it came time to go to the statewide orientation meetings, we took middle and high school teachers. When we had to decide whether we were going to become members of the league, we voted. Well, the middle school voted not to be in the league, and the high school voted to be in the league.

I determined that the reason was that the middle school folks thought the league would be more of all this stuff that they would have to do extra; you know, they had a gung ho principal (me) who was going to make them do a lot, . . . and we had done a lot that first year already. But if you throw something out the first year and nobody jumps on it, the time's not right. Then you bring it back up the next year, and maybe it makes some sense.

We heard rumblings that it was "just a conspiracy," and they [the administration] were "just going to ram it down our throats." So I kind of got the message that I needed to back off a little bit. And you know, the greatest idea in the world, implemented by the greatest leader or the greatest principal, is going to flop because it wasn't at the right time. How do you get a good sense of timing? It's just the school of hard knocks.

Frustrations, Obstacles, and Compensations

We asked Tommy what frustrations he feels and if he thinks he may still push too hard at times.

For some older teachers, the change has been more gradual, but I've been ready for 2 years to turn over more decisions to them, to let them decide who they are going to be on the team with or how they are going to group the kids. They hadn't wanted to do that; they wanted the administration to tell them how to do it. Well, we're evolving now after 3 years of this, and the staff development is helping get them in that frame of mind. But it's just a slow process. But if you've got it in your mind that the guiding principle is whatever you try to do, it needs to be better for kids, then you go try to do it. But, yeah, I worry sometimes about being perceived as being too ambitious. Now we've got somebody on the board who wants to change something at every meeting; that's good and it's bad.

One source of stress for me is the attitude of a teacher, for example, when we have bent over backward to tell everybody on the front end what is happening, we have communicated, we have gone through the whole 9 yards, and then that teacher (or teachers) stays on the other side of the issue. Somebody comes up and wants to change, or somebody didn't read the communications, or nobody lets me know something important. And then, when the thing is just about to reach culmination, here comes somebody who says they didn't really want that. This is when you've really made an effort to give them a shot, and you sat around and waited, but you didn't hear from them until three steps later when it's almost too far to go back and back up.

One of Tommy's self-reported weaknesses in regard to democratic governance is his tendency to ignore the "detractors or people with other viewpoints." He says:

Sometimes it involves a higher-up, and the central-office folks are coming around more to the fact that teachers need to have input. But I may not give [the detractor] as much of a hearing as to the people who are on my side. You know, you've got to listen and you know that, democratically, you're going to make a shared decision, and you can't let the way you feel about it affect their right to express their opinion, but . . . I'm doing better with that now. It's not as emotional or personal, and the action research helps. Still, you need to respect their opinions.

Listening to other viewpoints and resisting the urge to run on ahead of people has been a humbling experience for Tommy, but he steadfastly finds fulfillment in doing "what's right for kids, not what's going to make it easy for somebody else."

It's gratifying when I have wanted to do something for a long time but I didn't tell everybody, and either through staff development or something they heard at a conference, everybody decides it's a good idea. It's also great to see an idea through all the way from just talking about it at the start. I like seeing something I believe in for the kids come about. When I have high hopes and I think something's going to make a difference for kids and it does make instruction better, it gives me a great deal of satisfaction.

Nothing worth having has ever been easy. It's going to take a lot of work. And, you know, all the research will tell you it's hard to change. Nobody wants to change their little, safe environment; they may flop. But for me, the successes have been more than the lumps. So when you jump out there and get some things done and you feel like you're doing somebody some good, then it's not as hard to live with the frustrations and the other things that happen.

The two problems I see are time and communication, and the key word of a democratic leader is communication. It gets to be a question of whether it's worth it to sacrifice some of the things you've got to do to run the school every day, so you can look at some of these site-based initiatives. We've been able to keep the process going in a small enough amount of time that we haven't felt like we were being pulled away from other stuff. We haven't been consumed by the process, and we've been successful.

To Tommy, the future of democratic schooling is clear:

I think the school is going to be more of a site-based entity. I see teachers getting more involved in budget, staff development, classroom initiatives, and hiring personnel. We'll also get the teachers more involved in hiring—in order to have a mesh and mix of personalities for a team to be successful.

So Tommy Johnson goes forward, listening both to supporters and resisters, pushing gently, and watching his timing. Belmont County Secondary School seems to be coming into its own as a democratic school, led by a principal who constantly works at being "caring, concerned, and loyal to the staff."

Discussion Questions

1. What are Tommy Johnson's assumptions and beliefs about teachers' abilities, his role, and change in schools?
2. How are the visions or input of teachers, central-office personnel, board members, and Tommy Johnson linked to decisions made about this school?
3. What role do faculty meetings play in schoolwide decision making at Belmont County? What would you want to change about the meetings?
4. Does the democratic-governance initiative at Belmont County conform to your concept of democratic governance? What contextual factors enhance or inhibit this thrust?
5. Compare the democratic structures and processes at Belmont County with those of other schools. What advantages or disadvantages do you see in each?
6. To what extent do you think Tommy Johnson is perceived as a democratic leader by faculty, staff, and parents?
7. Do you agree with Tommy's tip to "stay tuned in, but bypass resisters"?
8. Is Tommy's "selective listening" compatible with democratic leadership?

8

"We're All in This Together"

Shared-Governance Experiences in a Middle and a High School

If a problem surfaces in our building, teachers have ownership of it—"OK, this is a problem. What are we going to do about it?" That's the attitude that exists, instead of the attitude, "Oh, my goodness, they've done this or they've done that, and all these terrible things are happening. What's wrong with these people? Don't they know what's going on?" Instead of complaining about a problem, our teachers have accepted ownership for it, and they know that we can solve it if we all work together.

—Robert Silver, Principal
Cloward Middle School

Robert Silver traces the development of his democratic orientation to his teachers union involvement early in his career. During his second year of teaching, he was elected president of the teachers association and was active in contract negotiations with the school board. This resulted in the early development of Robert's leadership skills and a commitment to representing the teachers' perspective in all administrative decisions.

> I definitely got interested in the idea of using the ideas of teachers. Even though our ideas weren't necessarily well received, the idea [of teacher involvement] was born in my mind. It made me really need to use the ideas of the people who work in the classrooms on a daily basis. They can help make some of the decisions that would be made, frankly, by people who don't always know what's going on in the classroom.

Robert, who is white, became principal at the young age of 26. His situation was unique in that he split his time between being a principal and a teacher in the same building. This is similar to the old "principal-teacher" model of the early 20th century, in which teachers were in charge of schools, and it contributed to his current commitment to bringing the teacher's voice to decision making.

Because Robert views the "quality interaction that occurs between the students and the teachers in the classroom" as central to a school's purpose, he believes that staff development is the key to a school's success. This would be a fairly conventional response were it not for the way that Robert conceives of staff development. True to his prior experience as an advocate for teachers, he views them as the "experts" who are the best source of ideas and innovations. He sees teaching, like all professions, as an ongoing learning process and views teacher learning as occurring within schools and among the teachers themselves:

> I would see teachers that had some tremendous ideas, but they were never shared. They stayed within that one particular classroom. I wanted to find a way to get those good ideas the teachers had and bring them out in the open so that everyone could benefit.

Pizza and Planning: Developing Trust

Robert feels that perhaps too much is made of school size. When he was first interviewed, Robert was the principal of Cloward Middle School, a suburban school with 890 students. Although at Cloward he promoted dividing the school into teams, or families of teachers and students, he believes that the key is found less in the size of the school and more in creating a safe-school culture in which teachers feel invited to communicate openly. How did he achieve this climate of trust in which teachers feel free to speak their minds?

> I just told the teachers that we were going to do some educational brainstorming and anybody who was interested should stay between the hours of after school and about 7 o'clock in the evening. I told them if they were willing to donate their time, I'd buy their pizza. And that's how we got started. We did some brainstorming sessions, and we started talking about the concept of involving teachers and that was the beginning point.

Responses from teachers to the idea of shared governance were mixed:

> Some people quite frankly said, "Look, it's the principal's job to make decisions," and almost accused me of abdicating my position. I explained to teachers that I don't have a monopoly on good ideas, and we have problems in education, we have problems in our building. I tried to tell them that I have a certain perspective on what the problem is, but, as teachers, they have a different perspective than mine; if I make the decision on how to solve this problem based on my perspective, I'm going to leave out some important considerations, and they can help me to learn what those considerations should be. So, we really approached it from a problem-solving perspective.

Robert initiated the "pizza-and-planning" meetings in 1989, well before his school's involvement with the League of Professional Schools. Because they had few examples of how to embark on shared governance, they began with relatively trivial policy issues, such as parking, lunch duty, and other matters with no direct effect on instruction. Since then, the group has gradually moved into high-impact areas, such as personnel selection, budget planning, and instructional methods. Robert insists that shared-governance structures cannot be simply brought into a school; rather they must be created on-site, as stakeholders design a system that fits their own local reality.

Changing Old Ways of Thinking

Robert found that one of his most difficult tasks was to help the teachers change their hierarchical view of decision making. They had been told what to do for so long that they instinctively fell back into old patterns, as he noted:

> People would come to me for money, or they would come to me to solve a problem, and they would expect me to be the one who alleviated that particular problem. The difference now is that it's a collaborative process. We identify problems, and the teachers, instead of coming to me saying, "Here, this is the problem. What do you want to do about it?" come to me and say, "We're having this problem and this is what we'd like to do." My role, instead of being the problem solver, is that I help stimulate ideas. I put them in touch with people who can come up with other ideas to help solve the problems. But we work collaboratively to solve problems, rather than by them bringing a problem and leaving it on my doorstep and then walking off.

Robert identified what he felt were cultural issues relating to teacher reluctance to give up a passive role in decision making. A midwesterner, he found that in the southern state in which he currently works, teachers do not have a strong union-organizing tradition. Unions, in spite of their many and well-documented shortcomings, have become in many parts of the country a forum for teacher leadership and teacher voice. According to Robert, although unionized teachers have been more aggressive about participation, they also have tended to perpetuate an "us-versus-them" labor/management relationship that militates against shared governance. He notes that as teachers unions and associations increasingly become partners in restructuring and shared governance, this posture has lessened.

Also, Robert sees a tendency of school hierarchical relations to reflect traditional family hierarchies, in which the male father/husband makes the decisions. Because teaching staffs in schools are largely comprised of women and because the socialization into the hierarchy is so pervasive, this relationship seems to be reproduced in schools regardless of whether the principal is male or female.

The only way to break down this conditioning of hierarchical decision making is to constantly model a trusting, participatory attitude toward decision making, as well as a belief in teachers' desire to do the best job possible. As Robert says:

> I have a lot of faith in teachers. I think teachers want to do a good job, and I think the act of trusting is an underlying principle of shared governance. You can't go into this with the idea that teachers are looking for the easy way out. I don't believe that at all. You know, your role as a principal is to help them find a way to do the good job that they want to do.

This trust allowed Robert to provide teachers with the tools that they needed to empower themselves. For example, he began by demystifying the school budget. He gave them copies of the school district's budget, taught them how it operated, formed a subcommittee to actually do the budget planning, and eventually completely turned over the budget to a teachers budget committee, which then made budget recommendations to the building leadership team.

Trust is also demonstrated in Robert's refusal to retain veto power. He asserts that if democratic principals retain veto power, it negates and undermines the entire system. A principal must believe that teachers will make the best decision, given both access to information and enough time to study an issue. This doesn't mean the principal has no role in decision making; the principal can serve as what Robert calls a troubleshooter during brainstorming, pointing out potential side effects of decisions or possible negative outcomes. Nor does it mean that principals do not retain some decision-making authority. For example, teacher evaluations are not a shared-governance issue, although forms of peer supervision and evaluation can and should be encouraged. There are also numerous delicate issues that students, parents, and teachers may not want to open up for scrutiny by others.

Trusting teachers to monitor themselves brings some beneficial effects. It improves morale and cuts down on what Robert calls "finger pointing" or blaming others for the school's problems. In contrast, the current attitude in Robert's school is that "we're all in this together" and "when problems arise, we seek solutions together." This shift from finger pointing to ownership of problems leads to a subtle form of positive peer pressure. Teachers begin to feel pressure to live up to high standards:

> I really think that in a building where you truly have a democratic environment and people depend on each other, teachers who are not carrying their weight are a burden to other members. They get more parent complaints. There's more student misbehavior in that teacher's class, and when the students leave that class and go to another teacher's class, it's a problem for that other teacher. Peer pressure is a major factor.

> Quite frankly, when I came to this building, the leadership from the teachers was negative. The teachers who were most vocal, who assumed the leadership roles, were not good leaders. I think the biggest thing about the democratic process and about shared governance is that the really skilled teachers have been able to rise to the top in terms of being leaders. And I think when you had an autocratic climate, really, the teacher who may have had the loudest voice was the one who prevailed, although he or she was not necessarily the one with the best ideas. Whenever everybody can be involved in considering ideas, then it's the people who have the best ideas who often rise to the top.

Conflicts, Risks, and Barriers
to the Democratic Process

Because schools are embedded within larger systems, the creation of a democratic culture will inevitably create some conflicts with other systems that are still managed in a more hierarchical, authoritarian manner. Traditionally, principals have had to deal with central-office politics, but previous to democratic management, issues were generally brokered individually. One of the often unanticipated side effects of empowering teachers is that they are willing to "take on" these other systems, often at great political cost to themselves or their principal. Recently, Robert and his teaching staff appeared en masse at a school board meeting to protest a decision that they felt would create overcrowding in their school. Although this cost Robert "a talking to" by the superintendent for breaking the chain of command, it demonstrated his willingness to take risks to live out his democratic principles. Robert explains it this way:

> I'm a social studies teacher, and I believe in the democratic process. The way things work in American education, the school board makes an awful lot of decisions about running the school district. School board meetings are open to the public. If the board is not getting the right information through other sources, then I believe that one of the ways that you can impact change in a school system is to go directly to the board. You have to believe in the democratic process to make shared governance work. Democracy is sometimes a very laborious process, but the strength of it is that you get a lot of different ideas into the melting pot. When democracy works the way it should, the more ideas you've got in there and the more open-forum discussions about the pros and cons of the ways to do things, then—I really believe that in the final analysis—you're going to come out with a decision that works best for everybody.

Besides the very real risks involved in democratic governance, there are also some barriers that have caused well-intended efforts by principals and teaching staffs to fail. Furthermore, once principals have worked with teachers to overcome past bureaucratic conditioning, even more barriers can become evident. Perhaps the most important is the issue of time. Robert admits that he and the teachers have yet to resolve this issue to everyone's satisfaction. Currently most shared-governance meetings at Cloward are unreimbursed and held after school hours. He would like to see more teacher-release time built into staff-development budgets and compensation given for the extra time teachers put in, drawing a parallel to the extra compensation coaches receive for after-school athletic programs. Recently the school was allocated a small income supplement that could be assigned to department chairs. Because the fine arts department is very small and the chair is already compensated as band director, it was decided, with the agreement of the fine arts chair, that the supplement should go to the chairperson of the building leadership team to help compensate her for her extra time.

Another barrier is a lack of system coordination. As an example of this, Robert cites short turnaround times demanded by central-office personnel for decisions made at the school level. Recently the assistant superintendent of finance sent Robert a copy of the school's budget for the upcoming year, on the basis of projected pupil enrollment, and gave Robert only a week to determine how the monies would be used. The shared-governance committee structure does not lend itself to such short turnaround times, which are premised on the image of a lone principal sitting in an office working out the details of a school's budget.

In spite of the problems associated with democratic governance, Robert finds many personal rewards in it. One of these is the professional collegiality that develops in shared-governance schools. He enjoys developing give and take with teachers and being able to "sit down and brainstorm problems in education, instead of feeling that there is a gulf between us." This sense of collegiality is accentuated when he and groups of teachers present their work together at local and national conferences.

Deepening the Impact,
Extending the Involvement

Although Robert sees important changes in the school's climate and culture, which he attributes to shared governance, he is less confident about its effect on classroom instruction. Shaking his head, he remarks, "Instruction is the last bastion. I think that's the area where we've got the most room to grow." What movement there has been in this area, he attributes to the inclusion movement in special education, in which regular and special education teachers work collaboratively. He believes, however, that the "we're-in-this-together" ethos that shared governance promoted made the transition to inclusion much smoother at Cloward than at other schools.

Besides facilitating decision making, Robert sees part of his new role as a generator of ideas, planting seeds that might find fertile ground within the school. He credits both professional reading and attending national conferences as sources of ideas.

Parents have not yet been integrated into the school's democratic decision-making process. Robert admits, "I'm not sure that my relationship with parents has changed a great deal through the move from a more autocratic to a more democratic leadership style." There are no parents on the building leadership team, but there is a school advisory committee made up of parents that has been in existence in the district for some time. In fact, these committees were mandated by the central office, and many principals simply use them as rubber stamps for what they want to do. According to Robert:

> To me, if you use your local school advisory committee in that way, it doesn't serve any purpose. In fact, I think there's a pretty strong case that can be built for putting your worst critics on your school advisory committee because that way they can learn more about the operational "ins and outs" of the school and at least understand why you're doing what you're doing. I say to teachers that people should look on criticism as an opportunity. It's an opportunity to learn how to do a better job.

The Freedom to Criticize

Robert stresses something that is often overlooked in accounts of democratic management: the issue of how safe people feel to criticize the principal and each other. Too often in apparently democratically run schools, teachers and students censor themselves because they feel that they might be marginalized in subtle ways if they speak with an authentic voice. Often when they do speak out, it is behind people's backs rather than to their faces. Robert insists that democratic leadership cannot flourish in a climate of fear:

> If teachers are fearful that if they say something to you that you don't like, you're going to somehow retaliate against them, then that'll kill the process. For democratic leadership to work, you have to have a completely free-flowing exchange of ideas. And teachers have to be comfortable with coming either to a principal individually or before a shared-governance body to say, "What we're doing here is not working."

Robert avoids this climate of fear, in part, by making sure that programs are not viewed as his own personal investment. When principals are personally invested in a program, a criticism of the program becomes essentially a criticism of the principal. Robert asserts that "the program at Cloward Middle School is our program. It's not my program, and if we change it, it's because our needs are not being met, ours including the students."

When the school decided to move toward the houses concept, in which cohorts of teachers and students could work together, the parents were brought into the process through the school advisory committee, which was used as a sounding board as decisions were made. Robert admits, however, that "that kind of involvement was typical even when I was making most decisions as the principal. I used the local school advisory committee as a sounding board for ideas. So, I don't know that that's really changed a lot. Parents have provided important resources." It was in large part because of extra funds provided by the Parent Teachers Association (PTA) that Robert was able to finance sending teachers to national conferences.

Advice From Empowered Teachers

When evaluators from the League of Professional Schools visited Cloward Middle School, teachers there gave the following advice to educators in schools that might be thinking of implementing a shared-governance process:

1. Understand that decisions made collectively will be better than those made individually, if the group has the information it needs. This is a basic premise of shared governance. If you don't believe this, don't try it.
2. Create an atmosphere in which people are willing to risk being wrong. Everyone should be encouraged to take risks. You can learn from your mistakes.
3. Have ample representation from all factions in the school.
4. Elect representatives to serve on committees; do not appoint them.
5. In general, do not select administrators to serve as chairs on committees.
6. Work toward consensus. Avoid voting; it can create hard feelings.
7. Do not let decision-making groups get too big. Discussions can go on forever without a decision being made.
8. Be careful. Teachers quickly get used to having a voice and will want involvement in more and more issues. Administrators should not start this if they do not really want it.

Democratic Governance
at the High School Level

Midway through our interview process, Robert was transferred to a high school within the district. He found some new challenges to democratic governance at the high school level. First, he found that high school teachers are more subject oriented and less accustomed to teaming and collaborating with each other. Middle school teachers who embrace the middle school philosophy

> tend to work more in teams, and they tend to do more hands-on kinds of things with the kids. When you have people who operate that way with students, they are a little bit more open to teaming together and to working together in a shared-governance process. So, I think it's probably easier

to initially work shared-governance ideas into a middle school that truly embraces a middle school concept.

Another issue that Robert encountered at the high school level was how to include the assistant principals in the democratic process. Including too many administrators on the building leadership team would create an imbalance, likely causing the meetings to be dominated by administrators. Robert's response was to have weekly administrative team meetings in which he could serve as a bridge between teachers and administrators. He reasoned that assistant principals might feel out of the loop and resentful if it were not for these meetings. Robert indicated that he could find little in the educational literature on the role of assistant principals in shared governance and that he viewed the current arrangement as workable until he could find a better way to include them in the process.

Having successfully created a democratic approach to decision making at Cloward Middle School, Robert is now creatively and confidently confronting new challenges to shared governance in a high school setting. He finds it hard to imagine being a traditional principal with its "lonely-at-the-top" image. His greatest sense of gratification comes from the collegiality that exists between himself and the teaching staff:

> As a democratic leader, my greatest satisfaction is the professional collegiality that I have with teachers. . . . I really feel that we are partners in solving problems. To me, that's been the biggest plus. When we go to things like the National Middle School Convention, where our school was chosen to make a presentation, I get a chance to interact with teachers as a colleague, not as a supervisor. To me that's the biggest part.

Robert thinks that the future of democratic schooling largely depends on whether principals will be able to relinquish their "narrow views of power and school administration" and then learn to understand and use power more appropriately:

I think so many people look on school administration as a power struggle. They think there's only so much power, and if you give up any, it diminishes your power. They don't understand that it's an exponential thing . . . and if you share it, it grows.

A New Superintendent

Regardless of how smoothly shared governance may seem to be going, there are always obstacles and potential setbacks. Recently, Robert's superintendent, whom he viewed as generally supportive of district reforms that included democratic governance, was asked by the school board to resign. As part of the agreement for her to leave her position, no one could talk about specific details of her departure. This left Robert wondering which of the reforms supported by the superintendent were viewed negatively by the school board and, by extension, the community. Robert was concerned that schools might be encouraged to reverse current reforms. He shared the following:

> I am concerned that one of the messages that may come out of the recent dismissal of the superintendent is that the climate here for innovative ideas is not very positive. I'm afraid. One of the real strengths of shared governance (and one of the issues we were dealing with early on when we started in the process) was that each school would kind of take on its unique characteristics. If you truly use the shared-governance process, then that means that the people in the school will determine what's important for them and they will pursue those particular issues. I think that one of the things that will probably come out of the superintendent's dismissal is more of an effort to try to say, "Let's not get so far apart in terms of what we're doing."

Robert is facing the fact that should this happen, he may be forced to decide whether his administrative ethos is compatible with the new district administration. If it turns out that the new superintendent wants to roll back the gains that Robert's staff have made toward democratic decision making, he and the staff will have to decide what to do. It is probably reasonable to assume that whatever their decision, it will be made democratically as colleagues confronting one more problem together.

Discussion Questions

1. What are some of the obstacles that Robert has had to overcome in attempting to implement a democratic leadership approach? What can principals do to provide more time for faculty members to collaborate?

2. What types of risks has Robert taken in promoting participatory decision making?

3. Review the suggestions that the teachers made for schools considering the implementation of shared governance. Do you agree with these suggestions? Why or why not?

4. Robert Silver is faced with a difficult decision if the new superintendent intends to roll back the gains made toward shared governance. Do you think that shared governance can be carried out in districts in which it is not supported by central-office administrators?

5. How does Robert's concept of power relate to his philosophy of shared governance?

9

Learning Democracy Together

Struggling With
Shared Governance
in an Elementary School

I'm sure that if I'm taken ill or decide to retire, the school is not going to go through some kind of convulsive freezing-up in which teachers declare, "Our leader's gone. What do we do now?" There are people here who would step forward and keep this place going. They would go to the superintendent and ask to be involved in selecting the next principal, so there would be a person here who would deal with them in a similar way.

—Richard Larkin, Principal
Stapleton Elementary School

Richard Larkin is the principal of Stapleton Elementary School, a recently built school in a medium-size southeastern U.S. city of 45,000 inhabitants. Stapleton has a student population of 575, 27% of whom are nonwhite. Richard, who is white, is a jovial man in his mid-50s with a warm personality and a lively sense of humor. As is the case with many democratically inclined principals, he worked as a teacher for principals who provided examples of what he did not want to become as an administrator. In past years, he worked for rigid, autocratic principals, as well as ineffective laissez-faire ones. Richard realized that he could do a much better job than the principals he worked for. This inspired him to return to graduate school for his administrative certification. Shortly after being certified, he was hired to be an assistant principal in a nearby high school. For 2 years he did nothing but handle discipline problems.

> I was put in charge of discipline, and that's all I did. I checked on the kids who weren't in class or who had been sent to the office for punishment, and I dealt with fights and students who were truant. There was a good bit of racial tension at the school, and I found that very unpleasant to deal with. My office was kind of like a doctor's office. After seeing a "patient," I'd go to the door, and there would be a long line of kids sitting on the bench waiting to see me. And teachers had the view that they were here to teach and to dish out all this knowledge and that it was somebody else's job to make them behave. I had that job for 2 years, and it was really a burnout experience.

Tired of hierarchical forms of administration that were oriented more toward issues of control than issues of instruction, Richard decided to apply for an administrative opening in a small elementary school in the same city. His application was accepted, and he subsequently spent 14 years as principal of Bowen Elementary School. When Stapleton was built in 1987, he moved there with a large contingent of the Bowen teaching staff. In recent years he has been able to recruit many creative and intelligent teachers to Stapleton.

Creating Structures for Participation

At Stapleton, a formal decision-making process exists whereby teachers communicate their concerns through small discussion groups to a leadership team that serves as a policy-making body. The leadership team changed its name to "Faculty Representatives" this year in response to negative feedback from some teachers who felt that the group was elitist. Although members were originally appointed by the principal, more recently the team has been open to anyone who wishes to volunteer. As a result, the team is actually what Richard calls a "y'all come" team rather than a representative body. Recently a plan to elect five representatives has been proposed. As yet, the idea of including parents and/or students on the team has not arisen.

Not all teachers are equally excited about giving their time to schoolwide decision making. As Richard points out:

> There are teachers on this staff who really don't want to be involved in the day-to-day management of the school. They have their classroom to take care of, and, I'm sure, they feel it's all they're capable of doing. Their heads are barely above water sometimes, and I know and can sympathize with that feeling.

> However, most of the people here—and I can't tell you why—really enjoy having a voice in how the school operates, and we most definitely do all have a voice. I am the principal and have a lot of authority, but the way I like to be perceived—and I think I am by most of them—is as just another person on the team. Sometimes I am the one who has the key to the door, but other than that, we're all equals. I ask for a lot of advice, and it's getting to the point, as we get into this process more and more, that I don't even have to ask. It comes unsolicited. And I think that's very healthy.

The shift to shared governance has not been easy. Richard and the teachers have had to keep each other on track in their journey toward democracy. There appears to be recognition on everyone's part that this is new and will require some renegotiating of roles. Much like contemporary marriages that struggle with changing gender roles, Richard and his teachers occasionally have to remind each other when they fall back into old patterns.

For example, Richard decided that it would be a good idea to have a teacher-of-the-month bulletin board. He thought it would be nice to "put somebody's picture up with a little biographical information and just try to make them feel good . . . get a little recognition." So he sent a teacher's aide to the lunchroom to prepare the bulletin board. At the next teachers meeting, Richard was confronted by teachers who wanted to know why they had not been consulted about it, who was going to pick the teacher of the month, the effect it might have on morale, and how it might encourage unhealthy competition among teachers. Richard describes his emotions after the meeting:

> Boy, my feelings were hurt, I don't mind telling you. I was sure they didn't have any trust in me. I thought they didn't trust me to pick someone who wasn't a favorite teacher of mine. But then I began to really reflect on it, and some other people I've shared this with said, "Well, it's a very healthy sign of your organization that 2 years ago nobody would have liked it any better, but they wouldn't have dared to say anything about it." Now there is more openness and a belief that we can have a voice in what happens in the school. In a meeting like that, it is really a healthy thing for a principal to be challenged and confronted.

This was an important learning experience for Richard, and from that time on, similar matters were decided as a group. As Richard points out, had the teachers not felt safe to challenge him on his unilateral decision, he would have been deprived of their feedback, and the school climate would have continued to be characterized by distrust and a lack of authentic communication.

Recently the teachers at Stapleton developed a "decision-making outline," consisting of a list of school issues and the persons who can make recommendations and who have the authority to act on the issues. This sheet was taken to the entire faculty who unanimously voted its approval. Teachers felt that the list was a significant accomplishment and that it has been an enabling factor in guiding decision making.

Although parents are not formally included in decision making and no formal parent advisory groups other than the PTA exist, Richard solicits parent feedback on potentially controversial issues. Last year, for example, the four kindergarten classes unexpectedly rose to 27 students per classroom. In consultation with the kindergarten and first-grade teachers, Richard considered moving a first-grade teacher to kindergarten and redistributing the first-grade children, but because the semester had already begun, parents did not want their children moved. Richard's letter to parents, indicating that they were considering the change, elicited a flurry of notes and phone calls.

> So we got together with the nine teachers and we took a look at the letters that had come in and the other kinds of feedback. We realized that we had gained enough in enrollment that we could hire an additional aide. We decided to leave everything the way it was and to add one more aide to the kindergarten classes. We communicated that to the people at the next PTA meeting, and when I made the announcement, the parents cheered loudly.

Ethical Leadership:
Trust, Honesty, and Openness

According to Richard, there are moral and ethical issues related to democratic leadership. Richard argues that there are certain attributes that are prerequisites for democratic leadership, such as trust, honesty, and openness, and that ethical leadership must be guided by these attributes. Trust is a constant theme among shared-governance principals, and Richard is no exception. Although he has always been a highly innovative principal with a strong human relations orientation, Richard finds initiating truly democratic structures to be a constant challenge. He, like other principals and teachers, has been conditioned by years of hierarchical school structures. These structures build management/labor types of relationships that often militate against the building of trust.

Some before-and-after shared-governance "snapshots" of Richard's leadership might help to illustrate how a nonhierarchical, open, and trusting climate changes the ways that innovation occurs in schools. In the "old" days before shared governance, Richard used his human relations skills to create an effective school that was both humane and instructionally innovative. He used the same

approach to leadership to get teachers to adopt teaching methods
that he believed in. He talks about how he got teachers to give up
basal readers:

> We were the first school that I know of in this area that went
> into a whole-language program. Now that's a buzz word, and
> it seems everybody's doing that, or at least they claim to be.
> Before whole language, a typical class would have three or
> four reading groups, and the teacher would have a circle and
> call all of them up to read, do a few pages in the workbook,
> and talk about a little skill of some sort. Then they would
> go back to their desks and do seatwork, and another group
> would come to the teacher. We were doing almost nothing
> with writing and some of the other things that go with lan-
> guage arts.

> At a reading conference I heard a presentation on a program
> called Success in Reading and Writing, which is a modified
> whole-language program started in the 1970s at Duke Uni-
> versity. I thought, "Gosh, this is the way schools ought to
> be." I came back from the conference and had a talk with the
> teachers about it. I was at the front of the room, and the
> teachers, of course, were dutiful subjects sitting at the tables,
> listening to what I had to say. I said, "If there's anybody here
> who's interested in this as much as I am, let me know and
> I'll be glad to buy you the manual for your grade level." One
> by one, teachers said, "You know, I think I'd like to have one
> of those." Then I brought in a person who had taught this
> method to do a little in-service at the end of the year.

> The last thing I said before they went home for the summer
> was, "When you come back in August, you will have a choice
> of going the traditional way we've taught, or you can choose
> to have a Success classroom next year." Every teacher who
> came back the next fall wanted to go with Success, every
> single one.

Most principals will recognize this as a successful leadership strategy within a hierarchical framework in which principals have the ideas and teachers need to be educated about new methods. Although Richard was successful in implementing the new method and teachers seemed to adopt it with little resistance, it remained more Richard's innovation than theirs. Contrast Richard's leadership in moving his school from a basal to a whole-language approach with the following change effort that took place within the more recent shared-governance framework:

> Trust just opened teachers up to their fullest potential. They began to get ideas and be creative. They figure, "Okay, we were allowed to do this little-bitty thing, maybe we can do something else." The first thing you know, you have teachers talking with each other, not about what they did last weekend or about the latest little piece of gossip. They're talking about instructional things—workshops they've been to, professional books they've read, ideas that they have.

> One of the most invigorating things that we do is something we do two or three times a year on an in-service day. We have a roundtable discussion in which there is no leader. We just sit down, and people start talking about the school. We've had some wonderful ideas come out of that. It just opens up people to their fullest potential. During these discussions, teachers start coming up with goals for the school. Recently they decided they wanted to have cooperative learning throughout the building. They talked about having people come in to train them and about some videos that some of them knew about. All this comes from them. They're enthusiastic about what they generate.

> Compare that to the usual approach in which the typical principal comes to a staff meeting and says, "Well, folks, I've decided we're going to have cooperative learning in every classroom, and you're going to go through this great training session." Well, some of them will do it dutifully, and some might even be excited, but there will be a lot of them

saying, "I'll show you. I might have to go to that training and I might have to watch that video, but I'm not doing any more than I want to." It's hard to get past resistance of that sort. You don't have that with democratic leadership. You have people who are enthusiastic, and they're thinking about how we can get better.

In this second snapshot, Richard is no longer the expert with the answers who must convince teachers of a good idea but rather a facilitator who creates and maintains a safe atmosphere for sharing ideas. Like the teachers themselves, he may alternatively move in and out of leadership and followership roles.

Approaches to leadership are also tied to the type of messages a principal gets from the central office. Richard has worked under two different superintendents. The first was very conservative and hierarchical; the second encouraged innovation and site-based management:

The former superintendent was so traditional and so conservative. He never wanted to see anything change, and he questioned everything you did. So under those circumstances, you don't venture out and put much at risk. Dr. Smith, the new superintendent, is extremely knowledgeable. He is much more of an open leader and gives you more freedom. In fact, under his leadership each school almost became autonomous and could do what it wanted as long as it was successful.

Besides trust, Richard believes that shared governance requires honesty and openness.

You have to be honest. If you're not an honest person, it's going to become evident very quickly. In a democratic organization, you can't get away with telling people you'll do one thing and then turning around and doing the opposite. In a democratic organization, communication is so good, you won't get away with that. People are going to tell each other what's happening and discuss how the place is run, so you have to be honest with people and not hold back things from teachers for their own good. You can't have a bunch of separate agendas that you're trying to accomplish and keep secrets from them.

Honesty is related to openness. You've got to be open to having people come in and tell you things you don't want to hear sometimes, upsetting though things may be. But that openness has got to be there. It's got to be part of what you do every day. You have to be viewed as approachable. Teachers aren't going to approach you if they think you're not honest, not listening to them, or that you don't want them to be there. If they get that sense, they won't come back, and you'll never know what they think.

Richard warns, however, that openness and honesty alone do not constitute good leadership. "I mean, you can be honest and open and be a fool, and you wouldn't be an effective leader. You've got to have leadership skills and consider the good of the school." What constitutes leadership in the context of shared governance has to do with facilitation, judgment, and turning followers into leaders, he suggests.

Positive Side Effects of Democratic Leadership

Richard also suggests that democratic leadership can be an answer to the stress that comes from the burden of shouldering all the responsibility and trying to be all things to all people. In this way many principals back themselves into an unhealthy role in which they become isolated and unable to enjoy collegiality. Richard finds his greatest reward to be the sense of collegiality that he has developed with teachers:

My greatest gratification is probably the people here. I just enjoy working with them so much, and when you have a democratic organization and you're part of it, it can be very rewarding. One of my old friends who was a colleague of mine in the 1960s used the phrase, "the admiral dines alone."

What he meant was that a lot of administrators don't expect anybody in the school to be their friend. If that were the way my day was here at school, then I wouldn't have any gratification. Frankly, I think there are some people who enjoy having power, enjoy making decisions by themselves. They enjoy making it hard on other people. Everybody knows somebody like that.

Not only is shared governance more healthy for principals and the school climate, but, contrary to popular belief, it is ultimately more efficient. This is because teachers are more likely to implement decisions that they have been involved in making. Richard describes how his teaching staff dealt with a recent decision by the legislature to have duty-free lunch periods for teachers. Richard called a meeting of the School Improvement Team. The teachers met in small grade-level groups and, after several meetings, came up with a plan for covering lunch duty that became a model in the district. According to Richard,

Under the old style of leadership that I had 5 or 6 years ago, I would have taken the yellow pad home at night and come up with a plan. It might have been a good plan, and it probably would have worked, but it would have been my plan. The teachers would have accepted it, but I would have gotten, "Oh, this stupid, duty-free lunch. Why do we have to do it this way? I hate this thing." This way, because the staff members were involved, I haven't heard a negative comment. It's worked well. The staff members were proud; they were going around patting themselves on the back. "Oh boy, this is a good plan; we did such a good job." Not long after that, we had people coming over here to see how we did it, because it was not working at their schools.

Perhaps my most important role in these meetings is just giving information. For example, somebody might say, "Does the law allow us to do that?" or "Is there a policy against that?" And my role would be to say, "Yes, there is," or "No, I don't know of any policy against it." And then they just make headway a mile a minute, but I'm not leading it. I'm not in charge of it, but I'm one of them in terms of making it come about.

Vulnerability to External Factors

A common concern is the extent to which innovations are vulnerable either to principal turnover or withdrawal of support by the superintendent and/or the school board. The current superintendent is highly supportive of Richard's shared-governance approach and has supported freedom for schools to experiment. In fact, this has created some unanticipated side effects.

> We went off in so many different directions it was like having six little private schools in town. It got to the point where people who weren't in this community were saying, "Well, why do they get to do that at Stapleton? Why do they have the whole-language program? Why can't we have one here?" Those kinds of questions were beginning to crop up in other communities and become almost uncomfortable for us.

Richard was encountering jealousy from other principals as the superintendent began to hold Stapleton up as the model for others to follow. Furthermore, one of the board members who is also the editor of the local newspaper had recently questioned whole language and shared governance. In many communities a backlash against progressive innovations is brewing, similar to the one against open classrooms in the 1960s. According to Richard,

> They've singled out things like cooperative learning and whole language. They've taken students' homework in which teachers haven't corrected misspelled words and put it on the front page of the newspaper. One thing they're particularly upset about is portfolio assessment. We did a pilot project on portfolio assessment last year. We didn't replace anything; we just did it as a pilot, but the feeling is out there that the school system is about to do away with report cards.

People think that we're going to let go of competition. One of the complaints against cooperative learning is that schools are being lowered to the level of the lowest child.

Richard worries that "it could be that with the wrong superintendent and the wrong board of education we could be told, 'You've got to stop doing those things'—things that have made us effective and innovative."

To further complicate matters, Richard's superintendent has just announced that he has accepted a superintendency in Virginia. All of these external factors demonstrate the fragility of shared governance at the building level. Although Richard indicates that he and the Stapleton teachers would "fight like cats and dogs" to defend what they have created together, without the support of the central office and the school board, any innovation is at risk.

The Future of Shared Governance

Nevertheless, Richard believes that democratic leadership and shared governance are here to stay:

Out of all the reform movements we've had, shared governance is the only reform that's got a chance to succeed because it's real, it makes a difference in the schools, and it comes from within the school. You can't just tell principals to go back to their schools and be democratic. You can't tell them that. It's got to spring up from some little seed or some kind of a willingness to do it. But once it does, it's a mighty powerful thing that can change the whole school. It can't come from state legislatures, and they cannot legislate curriculum and accountability. I mean they can do it, but it's not working. It hasn't worked here or anywhere else that I know of. What can create lasting change is when the people right down there at the very lowest level say, "By George, this is what we want to do at this school, and we're going to make it happen, and it's going to work because we're going to see that it does."

This shared-governance role makes the principalship a more doable job and creates an atmosphere of collaboration and collegiality that brings greater gratification to teachers and principals. A recent external evaluation of the school read, "Several teachers called the school 'teacher heaven,' although they cautioned that not everyone's personality would fit the school's philosophy and practice of shared governance." Richard seems aware that a "teacher's heaven" may or may not also be a parent or student heaven, but like so many other principals who experienced hierarchical, authoritarian systems, he feels sure that if teachers are involved and motivated, empowered students and communities cannot be far behind.

On a final note, Richard's feelings about the future of democratic schooling reflect both optimism and pessimism. On the one hand, he believes that only democratic approaches to schooling have a chance of succeeding. At the same time, Richard believes that many state legislatures and districts are misguided in mandating democracy in schools. He notes, "What can change the school is the people themselves, those at the lowest levels who want to do this. Only they can make this happen!"

Discussion Questions

1. Using the before and after "snapshots" of Richard's leadership approach, how would you characterize the differences between the two approaches?
2. Citing examples from this case, discuss the effect of the school's environment (i.e., central office, community, etc.) on the success or failure of shared governance.
3. Discuss the relationship of leadership to followership in a shared-governance model.
4. Richard notes that under the new superintendent a school "could do what it wanted as long as it was successful." What does this say about risk taking, experimentation, innovation, and democratic leadership?

10

Democratic Leadership
Lessons Learned

Principals' Backgrounds

Our findings indicate that personal and professional socialization dramatically affected the perspectives of the eight principals we studied. A range of personal experiences that contributed to their development as democratic leaders was reported. Tommy and Loretta described the influence of family members, particularly the recognition, confidence, and support they received. They learned the importance of giving respect and support to others and leading by example. Loretta and James described valuable lessons of former teachers who helped them to develop others, and Tommy learned the value of seeking input from his high school coach.

Other principals explained that their professional experiences as teachers contributed to their leadership orientation: Linda was a member of a leadership team, Tim chaired his school's faculty council, and Robert was president of a local teachers union. Tim, Tommy, Marcia, and Loretta also reported that mentoring by former participatory principals influenced them. As an assistant principal, Loretta worked for a strong principal who actively solicited input from the faculty, and Tommy, when he occupied the same position, learned much from participation on his school's leadership team.

Principals' Purposes

Melenyzer (1990) discusses three general approaches to teacher empowerment and school restructuring—conservative, liberal, and emancipatory. Conservative approaches (e.g., Maeroff, 1988) focus on the professionalization of teachers; liberal approaches (e.g., Glickman, 1993) include professionalizing teachers and enhancing teacher participation in schoolwide decision making, especially decisions relating to curriculum and instruction. The emancipatory approach (e.g., Giroux, 1992) emphasizes the critique of organizational and societal structures to enhance human possibility and democratic values, such as social justice and equality.

The purposes of the principals we studied were consistent with a liberal perspective on teacher empowerment and governance. Although the stated mission of the League of Professional Schools is "to promote the school as a learning community that is democratic, professional, and student oriented" (Program for School Improvement, 1993), at this point in time, shared-governance principals emphasize teachers' professional development and varying degrees of involvement in school-level decision making, especially about curriculum and instruction. School-governance structures have not yet achieved inclusiveness (parent and student participation is minimal) nor are democratic values directly and vigorously addressed. However, school democracy is an important goal of the league, and a handful of league schools have recently made important strides along these lines (L. Allen, personal communication, May 27, 1994). For example, in contrast to schools affiliated with the Oregon Network program (Conley & Goldman, 1994), school-place democracy and school improvement are primary purposes of shared-governance principals.

Empowerment and Shared-Governance Strategies

Several principals reported that letting go of power was a prerequisite to empowering others. The difficulty of letting go of traditional role identities (Bredeson, 1993) and sharing power with teachers in restructured schools has been discussed by others (Blase & Blase, 1994; Christensen, 1992; Prestine, 1991). Tim seemed to have little difficulty with this issue. He believed that a principal should relinquish all the power necessary to facilitate shared decision making. Referring to the E. F. Hutton phenomenon to highlight teachers' responsiveness to principals, he argued that "the higher you are on the chart, the less you need to say." Like several shared-governance principals, Tim refused to use a veto under any circumstances to countermand decisions made by teachers. These findings parallel those discussed by Goldman, Dunlap, and Conley (1991) and Leithwood, Jantzi, and Dart (1991).

Principals used a range of strategies to enhance teacher empowerment and to implement shared-governance structures and processes. Major strategies were building trust, encouraging expression, setting limits, hiring, encouraging group development, providing information, supporting teachers in confrontations, including parents/students, and using action research.

Building Trust

Trust has often been described as the cornerstone of successful shared leadership and teacher empowerment (Blase & Blase, 1994; Bredeson, 1989; Glickman, Allen, & Lunsford, 1994; Kirby & Colbert, 1992; Melenyzer, 1990). Overwhelmingly, the principals we interviewed argued that building trust with teachers was central to empowering them and implementing viable shared-governance structures in schools. Richard's efforts focused on developing a trusting school climate, and Robert constantly modeled trusting participative behaviors to break down teachers' previous conditioning into passive roles. Marcia's experience and knowledge of teaching helped to increase teachers' trust and respect for her judgment. (See studies by Brown, 1994, and Malen and Ogawa, 1988, for descriptions of the devastating effects of a failure to build trust by school principals in restructured schools.)

Encouraging Teacher Expression/Voice

In general, principals play a key role in the successful implementation of new school-governance structures (Blase & Blase, 1994; Duke, Showers, & Imber, 1980; Etheridge & Hall, 1991; Hallinger & Richardson, 1988; Murphy & Louis, 1994). Without exception, the principals we interviewed encouraged teacher expression/voice through the development of representative governance structures that deal with instructional and noninstructional, classroom and schoolwide problems and issues. Several principals reported that they created, in collaboration with teachers, leadership teams and ancillary structures for schoolwide decision making that were consistent with their unique situations. According to Brown (1994), individually designed approaches to governance allow schools to avoid what Barth (1990) called "list logic," that is, the idea that emulating another school's model of effectiveness will lead to effectiveness for a given school.

Marcia's streamlined approach to team decision making, which focused solely on curriculum and instruction, was designed to maintain school operations and allow teachers to teach. In contrast, Richard and Tim promoted the development of more complex formal and informal group structures through which teachers and administrators could communicate, brainstorm, problem solve, and make decisions about a wide range of issues. Several studies have described the link between viable governance structures and teacher expression/voice (Allen, 1993; Blase & Blase, 1994; Bredeson, 1989; Melenyzer, 1990; Reitzug, 1994).

In addition, principals made themselves approachable and accessible to encourage teacher expression. They explained that listening to teacher input and responding positively to teacher decisions facilitated expression. Principals also worked to create risk-free, safe-school climates in which teachers would not be criticized for what they said. The relationship between such leadership characteristics and the development of democratic structures in schools has been underscored in the work of others (Allen, 1993; Blase & Blase, 1994; Freeman, Brimhall, & Neufeld, 1994; Lindle, 1992; Melenyzer, 1990; Reitzug, 1994).

Robert sought to create a school environment in which teachers would not censor themselves and could openly and fearlessly express themselves. To avoid a climate of fear, Robert attempted to distance himself from proposals and programs. He believed that when principals are personally invested in specific programs, a criticism of the program often becomes a criticism of the principal. Of the principals we studied, Tim was the most emphatic in describing the vulnerability of school-based governance structures to changes in district and school-level administration; he underscored the importance of institutionalizing new governance structures in organizational policy.

Setting Limits

Several principals—Loretta, Tommy, Marcia, and Linda—set limits on teachers' involvement in decision making. In some cases, these principals vetoed teacher decisions or made unilateral decisions that they believed were in the best interests of students or the school as a whole. Researchers have found that such actions may have potentially adverse effects on teachers' willingness to participate in schoolwide decision making (Blase & Blase, 1994; Brown, 1994; Robertson & Briggs, 1993). Martin (1990) noted that traditional patterns of leadership that are controlling and regulating are counterproductive to empowerment efforts. However, principals can be expected to use the veto as long as they are held accountable for the outcomes of school-level decisions (Hallinger & Richardson, 1988; Prestine, 1991). By comparison, Robert, Richard, and Tim encouraged broader participation by teachers in schoolwide governance and typically refrained from using vetoes or making unilateral decisions.

Hiring

In general, the principals who participated in our study attempted to hire teachers who would fit into the new forms of governance and collaboration that were evolving in their schools. Marcia, for instance, hired new teachers who did not expect an authoritarian principal and would be able to get along with other faculty members. The principals we studied seldom included teachers in hiring processes, although some indicated that they had considered this. According to a League of Professional Schools spokesperson, 12 of 52 league schools now include teachers in hiring decisions in an advisory capacity (L. Allen, personal communication, May 5, 1994).

The school-restructuring literature is relatively silent with regard to teachers' participation in hiring decisions. In a study of schools in one district (Wohlstetter, Smyer, & Mohrman, 1994), teachers councils were permitted input in hiring; however, teachers were only allowed to respond to district-approved lists of candidates. The Chicago School Reform Act of 1988 has transferred major authority for hiring to local school councils composed of a principal, teachers, parents, and community members (Walberg & Niemiec, 1994).

Encouraging Group Development

Researchers have found that actions by shared-governance principals (e.g., building trust, listening, encouraging risk taking, communication) influence the development of teachers' groups (Allen, 1993; Aschbacher, 1990; Bredeson, 1989; Kreisberg, 1992; Lindle, 1992). Such actions affect the ability of groups to solve problems and the quality of decisions produced (Blase & Blase, 1994; Robertson & Briggs, 1993). Several of our principals reported that they actively facilitated group development of shared-governance structures such as teams and committees. Marcia explained that team building became necessary when new members cycled onto the leadership team. Tim pointed out that he avoided the manipulation of individuals and dealt with groups as a whole. According to Tim, playing off of individual teachers (and vice versa) could result in the unintended manipulation of a group.

Providing Information

Principals reported that their role in providing necessary information for team decision making was essential to shared governance. For example, Richard responded to faculty queries about resource availability and legal matters. Tommy communicated anticipated central-office-initiated changes and kept the faculty informed about his ruminations to avoid shocks. Robert often played the role of troubleshooter and pointed out potential side effects of decisions or possible negative outcomes.

The important role that principals play in facilitating the use and flow of information in restructured schools has been discussed by others (Robertson & Briggs, 1993; Wohlstetter et al., 1994). Blase and Blase (1994) found that providing professional articles and information about conferences enhanced teachers' sense of empowerment and ability to make informed decisions. Information from principals about restructuring and technical knowledge about school operations and information about how the components of reform interrelate also appear to increase teacher decision making (Murphy & Louis, 1994).

Supporting Teachers in Confrontations

Linda, Marcia, and Robert spoke directly about supporting teachers who were willing to take on their central-office administrators or school boards when district policies conflicted with what teachers considered was best for their schools. Linda described her faculty's successful stand against their school board's policy regarding self-contained gifted programs. Marcia commented on her faculty's application for "a variance to, of all things, the school calendar." Robert's faculty "appeared en masse at a school board meeting to protest a decision that they felt would create overcrowding in their school."

Including Parents/Students

Although the boundary-spanning activities of principals have expanded with school restructuring (Murphy & Louis, 1994) and principals tend to spend more time with parents and community and devote more time to public relations than before reform (Goldring, 1992; Hallinger & Hausman, 1993; McPherson & Crowson, 1994), studies provide only scant evidence that parents are formally and actively involved in school-level decision making. Malen and Ogawa's (1988) seminal study of site-based councils in Salt Lake City found that even though site-based councils had broad jurisdiction, formal policy-making authority, parity provisions, and training provisions, parents' influence was minimal. Among other things, principals tended to dominate decision-making processes.

In contrast, Wohlstetter et al. (1994) found that in "actively restructuring" schools (vs. struggling schools), principals communicated information to parents via newsletters and attempted to solicit parental input on some decision issues. Reitzug and Cross (1994) found that, in one of two restructured schools they studied, parents were actively involved in team decision making and there was "open dialogue" and "give and take." With the advent of reform in Chicago, decision-making authority has been transferred from the central office to local school councils that control hiring, firing, and school budgets (Walberg & Niemiec, 1994).

None of the principals we studied indicated that their schools substantially included either parents or students in decision making, although most acknowledged the importance of both groups. Robert mentioned that there was a school advisory team in all of the schools in his district, but he only used his as a sounding board. Some of the difficulties of creating partnerships with parents were discussed by Tim. Several principals, however, received parental feedback through informal means. Richard solicited parent reactions to potentially controversial issues. Only Marcia seemed to encourage limited student participation in decision making in addressing equity issues. Heterogeneous grouping and whole language were strategies that she employed to address such issues in the early grades. Linda, of course, discouraged student tracking of any type. Recently, a few

league schools have begun to include parents in decision making
(L. Allen, personal communication, May 5, 1994).

Action Research

Virtually all the principals we studied espoused the value of
using action research as a basis for shared decision making as advocated by the League of Professional Schools. This approach to research consists of collecting data from traditional sources (attendance
records, grades, test scores), conventional sources (surveys, interviews), and creative sources (student portfolios, demonstrations of
student learning, videotapes, exhibits) to make decisions, especially
about curriculum and instruction. (See Calhoun, 1994, for more information on the use of action research.) However, such approaches to
research in decision making appear to be limited in the schools
administered by the principals we studied.

A handful of other schools in the league have reported extensive
use of action research in making instructional and curricular decisions. Lack of time, inadequate knowledge, and the "mystique" of
research have limited its use in decision making (Calhoun & Allen,
1994). Little information about the use of action research in school
restructuring has appeared in the professional literature.

Additional Strategies

Selected principals described the use of additional facilitative
strategies. Tommy and Tim stated that honesty—a willingness to be
straightforward and to follow through on commitments—was critical to developing shared governance. Loretta linked caring to teachers' professional development. Both of these leadership characteristics
have been discussed in the school-restructuring literature (Allen,
1993; Blase & Blase, 1994; Bredeson, 1989; Kirby & Colbert, 1992;
Melenyzer, 1990). Tommy educated teachers who resisted democratic processes and relied on trusted teachers for another set of eyes.
James' remarks with regard to the central office—say what you need
to say—illustrate what Morris, Crowson, Porter-Gehrie, and Hurwitz
(1984) called "creative insubordination," that is, an approach to the

central office that is frequently employed by principals to protect and promote the welfare of their schools.

Outcomes of Shared Governance

Although studies of unsuccessful school restructuring point to serious negative outcomes for both principals and teachers (Bellon & Beaudry, 1992; Gitlin et al., 1992; Malen & Ogawa, 1988; Murphy & Louis, 1994; Reitzug & Cross, 1994), positive outcomes, consistent with those reported in the following paragraphs, have been linked to successful experiments in restructuring (Aschbacher, 1990; Blase & Blase, 1994; Bredeson, 1989; Freeman et al., 1994; Hallinger & Richardson, 1988; Melenyzer, 1990; Reitzug, 1994; Rice & Schneider, 1991).

Principals in our study described a range of outcomes—especially for teachers—that they believed resulted from their schools' involvement with shared governance. Teacher-related outcomes included improvements in classroom and schoolwide efficacy, influence in formal decision making (advisory and decisional), expression/voice, communication, problem solving, experimentation/innovation, risk taking (instructional, noninstructional), professional growth, leadership, morale, motivation, commitment to shared governance, sense of community ("we-ness," family/team feeling), assertiveness (vis-à-vis school boards), and team development.

Murphy and Louis's (1994) review of the restructuring literature underscores a range of problems confronting school principals. In contrast, our study emphasizes positive outcomes associated with relationships between principals and teachers—specifically, improvements in communication and collaboration, school efficacy, and the development of common visions. Positive outcomes for principals themselves related to motivation, commitment, satisfaction, openness, risk taking, facilitation (less manipulation/control), and a sense of belonging (decrease in isolation). Richard also argued that shared governance led to greater efficiency (compared with traditional governance), because teachers were more likely to implement decisions in which they were involved.

The professional literature is relatively silent with regard to the relationship between school restructuring and student learning. Several of our principals felt that shared governance resulted in positive outcomes for students; however, they seemed to be less confident about such outcomes. Student-equity outcomes were identified by two principals. In another study, Blase and Blase (1994) found that facilitative leadership and shared decision making positively affected teachers' classroom autonomy, reflection, motivation, and work effort.

Major sources of satisfaction for principals were linked to both shared-governance processes and outcomes. Principals derived satisfaction from the collegiality, camaraderie, and excitement that developed when people worked together on an idea to which all were committed. Tim stated that being partners in solving problems was the biggest plus. Marcia attributed her satisfaction primarily to being a "teacher of teachers" and seeing her staff "anxious to come back in August."

Principals' personal satisfaction was linked to being successful and seeing growth in teachers and programs. Tommy and Loretta talked about the pride that they and their faculties felt because of their achievements from working together. A high point for Loretta occurred when her faculty was involved in something that "someone else wants to hear about." No data about principal satisfaction have appeared in the research on school restructuring.

Relationships With the
Central Office and School Boards

Our principals reported that central-office administrators and board of education actions and policies significantly influenced shared governance at the school level. (This is particularly interesting in light of theoretical work that contends that decisions made at the higher levels in school organizations have little impact at the building level [Bidwell, 1965; Weick, 1976].) Such effects have received mixed reviews by the principals described throughout this book. Several stated that their superintendents were generally supportive of their work in shared governance; however, only in Loretta's case was such support noticeably active and predictable.

Wohlstetter et al. (1994) found that in some of the districts studied, superintendents actively worked to create teacher involvement in school-level decision making by supporting school changes, reducing central-office hierarchy, and encouraging risk taking. In one of two districts studied, Smylie and Crowson (1993) found that the central office supported restructuring by providing staff development to build both teacher-principal collaboration and understanding and acceptance of new decision-making structures.

Marcia and Loretta noted that system parameters constrained discretion and action at the school level and in some cases contradicted espoused support. Robert was reprimanded by his superintendent for supporting his staff in a confrontation with the school board; he was also accused of abdicating his responsibility as principal for permitting teacher involvement in budget planning. Tim reported that a basic ethical understanding between himself and the central office helped him to "walk that line among ethics, values, your belief system, and political expediency."

Other difficulties with the central office seemed to be a function of bureaucratic organization. For example, Robert explained that short turnaround times made it difficult for teachers to meet and address budgetary matters. In addition, difficulties associated with superintendents' succession were apparent in the data. In certain cases, terminations and resignations provoked deep anxiety in principals about the fate of shared governance at their schools. For instance, Robert and Richard worried that the achievements of shared governance were at risk with the arrival of new superintendents.

Other difficulties for principals described in the available research literature relate to the central office's inclination to, on the one hand, mandate site-based decision making for schools and, on the other hand, to maintain a top-down orientation (Education Commission of the States, 1990). Problems of accountability—that is, principals are accountable for school-level decisions, but such decisions are made by others—and role ambiguity are also described in relation to the central office (Hess & Easton, 1991). Smylie and Crowson (1993) discovered that central-office personnel frequently neglected to clarify questions about accountability and failed to develop new principal performance criteria, even though the role had changed.

Principals were also caught between traditional central-office expectations and teachers' new expectations for participation in decision making. Brown (1994) found that the central-office personnel's unwillingness to clarify teachers' roles in decision making resulted in skepticism by teachers about whether decisions would be supported. Insufficient time for decisions and failure to allow teachers to have authority in making major curriculum changes led to declines in commitment and trust.

For most of the principals we studied, relationships with school boards were problematic. In some instances, overt political action by groups of teachers was successful in challenging board decisions that contradicted school-level considerations. James stated that he would challenge any rule that contradicted his school's efforts in shared governance, but not in a malicious way. Tommy was admonished that listening to teachers would get him into trouble. Richard explained that one board member, a local newspaper editor, questioned the idea of shared governance and innovations such as whole-language instruction.

Barriers to Shared Governance

Principals described potential and actual barriers to shared governance, including those related to self, time, teachers, and higher-ups (superintendents, central-office personnel, school boards).

Self

Barriers identified with principals themselves were discussed by Tim, Tommy, and Richard. They recognized the absolute necessity of learning to let go of power to make shared governance work; however, they admitted to particular difficulties along these lines. For instance, Tommy explained that he had an urge to run the school and tended to push too hard at times. After a confrontation with his staff about his proposed teacher-of-the-month bulletin board, Richard learned that letting go was indeed more difficult than he had realized. Relatedly, Tommy reported that he had a tendency to rely on the viewpoints of trusted teachers and to ignore teachers that he believed were detractors of shared governance. (For more about the difficulties of letting go, see the work of Blase & Blase, 1994; Bredeson, 1993; and Christensen, 1992.)

Time

Blase and Blase (1994) and Reitzug (1994) have found that providing time to teachers is an essential factor in giving them voice and actualizing the results of their reflection/critique. Nevertheless, many of the principals we studied reported that shortages of time were a major barrier to shared governance. The problematic nature of time is discussed throughout the restructuring literature (Allen, 1993; Blase & Blase, 1994; Bradley, 1992; Bredeson, 1989; Peterson & Warren, 1994; Reitzug, 1994).

Robert explained that governance meetings were not reimbursed and they were held after school. Tim and Linda indicated that there was not enough time to deal with all decisions; Linda said that her most active teachers were beginning to get burned out. Tim's remarks highlight a well-known truth shared by our principals: Transforming organizational and cultural structures requires a great deal of time over the long term. This finding is consistent with other studies of school restructuring (Aschbacher, 1990; Blase & Blase, 1994).

Teachers

Not surprisingly, teachers' traditional expectations for principal behavior were a major barrier for shared-governance principals. Typically, teachers have been socialized into the norms of bureaucratic organization and subordinate compliance (Blase, 1988; Lortie, 1975). In fact, Malen and Ogawa (1988) attributed part of the failure of site-based decision making to teachers' traditional respect for and deference to principals' authority and expertise. Loretta, Tim, Robert, Linda, and Tommy reported that some teachers wanted them to employ a traditional approach to leadership—to define expectations, develop plans, solve problems, and, in general, make decisions for the school. Tim noted that some teachers almost accused him of abdicating his responsibility. Linda indicated that she probably should have been more autocratic during her first year; she believes that teachers are very territorial, unable to see the entire school, and have been socialized into antidemocratic behaviors.

Superintendents, the Central Office, and School Boards

Earlier in this summary, superintendent succession (resulting from terminations and resignations) was identified by several principals as an impediment to shared governance. For example, Richard disclosed that his superintendent's resignation resulted in ambiguity and uncertainty and placed his school's work in shared governance at great risk.

In a few cases, principals complained that negative attitudes by central-office administrators as well as bureaucratic factors (e.g., short turnaround times) negatively affected shared-governance efforts. Robert stated that district-level administrators viewed teacher involvement in budget decisions as an abdication of his responsibility as principal.

Other principals directly discussed barriers associated with school boards. Recall Richard's difficulties in dealing with one board member who questioned the ideas of whole language and shared governance.

Additional barriers to shared governance noted by principals included problematic economic conditions, the constraints of state standards, lack of institutionalization of new governance structures, inadequate initiation and implementation plans, poor communication, resentment of other district principals, teacher burnout, and the development of factions within faculties.

The Future of Democratic Schooling

Some of the principals we studied were decidedly optimistic about the future of democratic schooling. Linda argued that dealing with 21st-century needs would require more inclusive approaches to governance and that such approaches have already received sufficient support in the larger society. However, most of the principals in our study were more tentative about the future. They believed in the efficacy of school-based democracy, especially its capacity to encourage risk, experimentation, and innovation to, as Loretta noted, search for new ways to serve the needs of children. Nevertheless, these principals also realized that support for experimentation in various forms of shared governance from state legislatures, school district offices, and school boards was not assured.

The Discourses of Teacher Empowerment and Democratic Schools

The terms *empowerment* and *democracy* have entered educational administration discourse with little attention to the extensive theorizing about issues of power and democracy over the years. From the representative democracy of Native American confederations, which were the conceptual genesis of the U.S. Constitution, through the "lived democracy" of John Dewey, to contemporary critical theorists' conceptions of strong and critical democracy (Barber, 1984; Goodman, Kuzmic, & Wu, 1992), we have struggled with what it means to create democratic ways of life. Similarly, theorizing about power and empowerment has a long tradition from Machiavelli's *The Prince* through Freire's *Pedagogy of the Oppressed* and current political scientists' discussions of the various dimensions, or "faces," of power (Bachrach and Baratz, 1970; Lukes, 1974).

The principals that are discussed in this book have adopted the currently fashionable language of empowerment and democracy to describe their work with teachers. Although this language may not carry the intellectual imprint of centuries of social theory, it does reflect lived experience in the political force field of American public schools. Grounded in the day-to-day reality of school life, the eight cases in this book reveal the musings of principals as they reach for ideals of democracy and empowerment in diverse settings and share their successes and failures. In these cases, the idealism contained in much of the current writing on school democracy and teacher empowerment is tempered by the obstacles, contradictions, and complexity of moving schools toward these goals, no matter how limited their definition.

We argue that participatory discourse is overshadowed by administrative discourse and that its emancipatory intent often becomes distorted into an alternative technology of control. Too many school administrators are adopting the discourse of participation even though they have power-over mind-sets. What sets the eight principals in this book apart is their authentic commitment to pushing the ideals of democracy and empowerment as far as they can within systems that are characterized by power-over attitudes. These cases demonstrate that even when superintendents are sympathetic, the system throws up daily bureaucratic and political obstacles to democratic decision making at the school level.

Discourses on Decision Making

Three kinds of discourse are evident in discussions of school-based decision making: teacher professionalism, teacher participation, and teacher empowerment. The first (and most conservative), teacher professionalism, addresses what Maeroff (1988) refers to as the crisis of confidence in teaching. Within this discourse, teacher empowerment refers to gaining more professional respect for teachers, comparable to the respect of professionals in law and medicine, who are viewed as acting from a specialized and technical knowledge base. This discourse seeks better working conditions for teachers by focusing on how professional expertise results from reflective practice (Schon, 1987), improves the quality of the school as a workplace, and affects the classroom (Lieberman, 1988). Although the teacher-as-professional discourse has addressed important issues, it generally does not embrace a broad participatory orientation. The subtext of teacher professionalization reinforces a lay-professional division and often exacerbates the resentment that many teachers feel about parental participation in decisions about their children's education. Thus the discourse of teacher professionalization often precludes significant participation by others in school decisions.

A second prominent discourse is referred to as teacher participation in decision making (Glickman, 1993). Earlier, following Melenyzer (1990), we referred to this discourse as a "liberal" orientation. Teacher participation is incorporated in decision making, both as a way for teachers to gain more power over their classroom and work life (thus the notion of empowerment), as well as for them to gain a voice for the types of expertise that teachers have acquired within a school. This expertise includes both the professionalism at the core of the discourse and the local knowledge that teachers possess of their workplace and their students. Thus teacher participation allows the teacher's voice to inform school policy making.

However, this discourse usually assumes a hierarchical school system that is not affected by the larger social reality. Because of this condition, empowerment requires an agent, usually a principal or superintendent, who allows teachers to have more power. Of course, power that can be given can also be taken back, as we have observed in a few of the cases in this book. And too often this power is not extended to the community or to issues of equity that have ramifications beyond the confines of the school and classroom.

A third discourse is teacher empowerment. Although the term *empowerment* has been used to describe the previous two discourses, we wish to use the original, more circumscribed definition of social theorists like Freire (1970). According to this model, power is neither a privilege given by a superordinate agent nor a zero-sum game in which teachers acquire power at the expense of others. Rather, power is exercised with others in collaborative efforts that include students and have the students' welfare at their center. Keith (1994) views participation as an ethical imperative in teacher empowerment. It is

> rooted in the fundamental human right of agency—the power to work collectively and interdependently with others to co-construct our world. It is premised on limiting and eventually eradicating power differentials and inequalities and reconstructing the workplace, school, and other organizations as just and caring democratic communities. (p. 8)

The empowerment model requires that democratic processes lead to democratic outcomes. In other words, schools are not democratic if they engage in shared governance but are structured nondemocratically through academic tracking and other discriminatory practices on the basis of the social class, gender, race, or sexual orientation of parents and students.

All three of the discourses on school-based decision making are present in the cases reported in this book. However, although all of the principals we studied adhered to strong notions of teacher professionalism and teacher participation, they place less emphasis on teacher empowerment. The lack of a broad empowerment discourse cannot always be attributed to principals and teachers. In fact, there are many obstacles to achieving democratic, empowered schools.

Obstacles to School
Democracy and Empowerment

One such obstacle is the diverse and often contradictory motives that decision makers at all levels of the school system have for supporting teacher participation. Some view the devolution of decision making to lower levels of the hierarchy as a way to disperse responsibility for unpopular decisions during a time of retrenchment and crisis (Anderson & Dixon, 1993). Thus some superintendents and principals may simply wish to hand off crisis and stress to a staff or community level.

In other cases teacher participation may represent an alternative means to achieve administrative controls. In a human relations model, teacher participation may be limited to the satisfaction of teachers' psychosocial needs, including affiliation and self-esteem. Here, power is viewed as a privilege rather than a right and can be taken away at any time. Robert (see Chapter 7) is facing such a possibility as he waits to see whether the new superintendent, driven by school board distrust of progressive innovations, will roll back the move toward participation at his school. Ironically, the lack of community empowerment in his definition of democracy might have allowed a handful of conservative parents to pressure the school board on these issues.

Conclusion

The transition from teacher participation to teacher empowerment will require changes in what Reitzug and Capper (1993) call the scope of authority (degree of discretion provided), scope of involvement (to whom authority is distributed), and scope of influence (to which issues authority is delegated).

To move the scope of authority from participation to empowerment, shared-governance structures must be more than advisory, principals should not have veto power, and district and state policies must be waived when appropriate. To make a similar shift in the scope of involvement, all constituencies of the school must participate in decisions; this includes students, parents, and community groups. However, as discussed previously, even with all of these constituencies represented, power differentials will prevail in subtle ways (see Malen & Ogawa, 1988). To move the scope of influence from participation to empowerment, all issues must have the potential to be turned over to shared-governance groups—even core decision areas related to budgets, personnel, and programs.

The principals and teachers in this study are a long way from empowerment in its strongest sense, but they are enthusiastically moving in that direction. Furthermore, as several of the principals we studied pointed out, there is no way to rush school democracy and empowerment. Progressive superintendents and principals who try to mandate participation—an increasingly common practice—are ignoring decades of research on the top-down implementation of innovation and change. By definition, democracy and empowerment must be created at the bottom, and although they can be nurtured and fostered from the top, they cannot be mandated. After 3 years of experimentation, these principals and the teachers with whom they work have come a long way in laying a strong foundation for democracy and empowerment. It remains to be seen what the house they build will look like. We hope to be around for the housewarming.

Resource A

Research Methods and Procedures

This book portrays principals' challenges and practical approaches to democratic leadership in a variety of schools that are members of the League of Professional Schools. For readers interested in understanding the methods and procedures used to gather the data on which the book is based, a description is provided below.

The League of Professional Schools: Background

As members of the League of Professional Schools, we studied principals in eight schools that began implementing shared-governance structures and action research protocols during the fall of

1990. The league's purpose is to establish representative, democratic decision-making structures to promote teacher involvement primarily in schoolwide instructional and curricular decisions. Governance structures often deal with topics such as staff development, educational materials, program innovation, classroom management, scheduling, budgeting, hiring, and textbook adoption. Action research involves school staff members in collecting, analyzing, and interpreting data to assess the effects of shared decision making on students, teachers, administrators, and parents and to improve decision-making processes and outcomes.

The League of Professional Schools does not specifically prescribe how member schools should realize their commitment to shared governance. Each school is encouraged to create policies and procedures that fit its unique situation. Membership in the league provides (a) opportunities to network with other schools at periodic meetings involving teams from all league schools; (b) a biannual network exchange newsletter; (c) access to an information retrieval system for information relevant to instructional initiatives; (d) planning, evaluation, research, and instrumentation services via telephone; and (e) a yearly, on-site visit by either a league staff member, university associate, or league practitioner.

Schools interested in league membership send a team (usually three teachers and the principal) to a 2-day orientation and planning workshop in which the central premises of the league—shared governance and action research—are described in the context of instructional and curricular issues. Based on this information, staff members of a given school vote (by secret ballot) on becoming league members. An 80% favorable vote is required before schools are eligible to join the league. Using similar voting procedures, each school decides either annually or semiannually whether it wants to continue membership in the league.

The Study

Participant Selection Process

Based on recommendations of the League of Professional Schools participants and facilitators, Georgia State Department of Education personnel, and University of Georgia faculty working with the league, a pool of 45 possible participants was selected. Recommendations were based on reports of a principal's effectiveness and modeling of democratic leadership principles in a public school setting in Georgia.

Demographic data were compiled for each of the 45 candidates. Eight principals were selected for participation in our study on the basis of the goal of achieving the broadest possible representation of race and gender and on school-setting diversity across the elementary, middle school, and high school levels. The study sample consisted of male ($n = 5$) and female ($n = 3$) principals from rural ($n = 3$), suburban ($n = 3$), and urban ($n = 2$) school locations. Elementary ($n = 3$), middle school ($n = 2$), and high school principals ($n = 3$) participated. The average age of participating principals was 50; the average number of years in a leadership position was 7. Degrees earned were Ed.S. ($n = 6$) and Ed.D. ($n = 2$). Two alternate participants were also selected. Each principal was then contacted by the researchers, and the scope and purpose of the study were explained. All eight agreed to voluntary, noncompensated participation in the study.

Data Collection

Data collection and analysis were consistent with symbolic interactionist theory. Although this theoretical approach recognizes that structural factors influence action, it emphasizes the meanings that people assign to action. In other words, people's reflexivity is given more importance than structural factors. As a product of social action, the individual is influenced but maintains sufficient distance from others and is capable of initiating individual action (Blumer, 1969; Mead, 1934). Symbolic interactionism, in contrast to some qualitative research orientations, stresses individual perception and interpretation (Blumer, 1969; Tesch, 1988). Therefore, the study reported in this book investigated the broad question, What are principals' perspectives on democratic leadership in schools? An initial protocol of open-ended interview questions regarding the nature and practices of democratic leadership was developed by the researchers. The questions explored the principals'

1. personal development as democratic leaders over their professional careers
2. purposes/goals of democratic leadership
3. strategies/techniques used to enact democratic leadership
4. major problems and crises that principals have confronted as democratic leaders
5. major sources of stress/failure, gratification/success
6. values/ethical issues related to democratic leadership
7. impact of actions on others (particularly teachers and students)
8. relationships with central-office personnel (and parents, community members) and how such relationships helped/hindered democratic leadership
9. projections of the future of democratic leadership and democratic schooling

Data collection took place over the 6-month period between June and November of 1993. A researcher spent up to 6 hours in site-based and telephone-based conferences with each participating principal.

Initial interview dates were scheduled, at the principal's convenience, with seven of the eight principals at their school sites. (One principal preferred to come to the investigator's office due to obligations in the area.) Prior to the beginning of the interview, each principal completed a personal history questionnaire and an essay-style questionnaire regarding the characteristics of the district and school in which the principal practiced. Two principals were in transition between positions and therefore included information for both schools/districts. The initial interviews followed the open-ended protocol questions but also allowed follow-up and clarification as needed. The interviews were audiotaped by the researcher; initial interview times ranged from 2 to 4 hours in length.

Following each interview, audiotapes were reviewed for quality and professionally transcribed. Researchers then reviewed transcriptions for accuracy and began initial analysis of the set.

An initial review of the data focused on data completeness and areas of needed clarification within and across cases. The researchers designed the second protocol of interview questions for each individual case study to clarify and extend information within and across the cases and to elicit information regarding patterns that had surfaced during the initial round of interviews.

The second set of interviews was conducted by telephone. Each interview followed its individual question protocol and ranged from 1 to 2 hours in length. At its conclusion, a researcher briefly queried the participant to clarify, expand, and elaborate portions of the interaction, as well as to provide an opportunity for the participant to ask questions or express concerns regarding the study. Each of these interviews was audiotaped and transcribed.

Data Analysis

Interview data were analyzed according to guidelines for grounded theory inquiry and constant comparative analysis (Glaser, 1978; Glaser & Strauss, 1967). This approach to analysis requires a comparison of each new unit of data to those coded previously for emergent categories and subcategories. Specifically, data related to each of the research questions were clustered for each individual principal studied as well as for all eight principals. The latter procedures produced the categories and themes across the database and served as a basis for developing the summary statements discussed in the final chapter of this book.

Questions that yielded limited data are not discussed in this book. However, the absence of data should not be construed to indicate the relevance or nonrelevance of a particular topic or issue for a given principal. The interview protocol only explored topics and issues that the principals themselves identified. Data from interviews have been used throughout to illustrate selected ideas (quotes have been edited slightly for succinctness and clarity). To preserve principals' anonymity, pseudonyms have been used.

References

Allen, L. R. (1993). *The role of voice in shared governance: A case study of a primary school.* Unpublished doctoral dissertation, University of Georgia.

Anderson, G. L. (1991). Cognitive politics of principals and teachers: Ideological control in an elementary school. In J. Blase (Ed.), *The politics of life in schools: Power, conflict, and cooperation* (pp. 120-130). Newbury Park, CA: Sage.

Anderson, G. L., & Dixon, A. (1993). Paradigm shifts and site-based management in the United States: Toward a paradigm of social empowerment. In J. Smythe (Ed.), *A socially critical view of the self-managing school* (pp. 49-63). London: Falmer.

Argyris, C. (1982). *Reasoning, learning and action: Individual and organizational.* San Francisco: Jossey-Bass.

Aronstein, L. W., Marlow, M., & Desilets, B. (1990). Detours on the road to site-based management. *Educational Leadership, 47*(7), 61-63.

Aschbacher, P. R. (1990, April). *School restructuring: Towards teacher empowerment.* Paper presented at the annual meeting of the American Educational Research Association, Boston.

Bachrach, P., & Baratz, M. (1970). *Power and poverty.* New York: Oxford University Press.

Ball, S. J. (1987). *The micro-politics of the school: Towards a theory of school organization.* London: Methuen.

Barber, B. (1984). *Strong democracy: Participatory politics for a new age.* Berkeley: University of California Press.

Barth, R. S. (1988). School: A community of leaders. In A. Lieberman (Ed.), *Building a professional culture in schools.* New York: Teachers College Press.

Barth, R. S. (1990). *Improving schools from within: Teachers, parents, and principals can make a difference.* San Francisco: Jossey-Bass.

Bates, R. (1986, April). *The culture of administration, the process of schooling and the politics of culture.* Paper presented at the annual meeting of the American Educational Research Association, San Francisco.

Bellon, T., & Beaudry, J. (1992, April). *Teachers' perceptions of their leadership roles in site-based decision making.* Paper presented at the annual meeting of the American Educational Research Association, San Francisco.

Bennis, W., & Nanus, B. (1985). *Leaders: The strategies for taking charge.* New York: Harper & Row.

Bidwell, C. (1965). The school as a formal organization. In J. G. March (Ed.), *Handbook of organizations* (pp. 972-1021). Chicago: Rand McNally.

Blase, J. (1988). The everyday political perspectives of teachers: Vulnerability and conservatism. *Qualitative Studies in Education, 1*(2), 125-142.

Blase, J. (1993). The micropolitics of effective school-based leadership: Teachers' perspectives. *Educational Administration Quarterly, 29*(2), 142-163.

Blase, J., & Blase, J. R. (1994). *Empowering teachers: What successful principals do.* Thousand Oaks, CA: Corwin.

Blumberg, A., & Greenfield, W. (1980). *The effective principal: Perspectives on school leadership.* Boston: Allyn & Bacon.

Blumer, H. (1969). *Symbolic interactionism: Perspective and method.* Englewood Cliffs, NJ: Prentice Hall.

Bolin, F. S. (1989). Empowering leadership. *Teachers College Record, 91*(1), 81-96.

Bradley, A. (1992). New study laments lack of change in Chicago classrooms. *Education Week, 11*(27), 1, 19.

Bredeson, P. V. (1989). Redefining leadership and the roles of school principals: Responses to changes in the professional work-life of teachers. *High School Journal, 23*(1), 9-20.

Bredeson, P. V. (1993). Letting go of outlived professional identities: A study of role transition and role strain for principals in restructured schools. *Educational Administration Quarterly, 29*(1), 34-68.

Bridges, E. M. (1982). Research on the school administrator: The state of the art. *Educational Administration Quarterly, 18*(3), 12-33.

Brown, D. F. (1994, April). *Experiencing shared leadership: Teachers' reflections.* Paper presented at the annual meeting of the American Educational Research Association, New Orleans, LA.

Calhoun, E. (1994). *How to use action research in the self-renewing school.* Alexandria, VA: Association of Supervision and Curriculum Development.

Calhoun, E. F., & Allen, L. (1994, April). *Results of schoolwide action research in the League of Professional Schools.* Paper presented at the annual meeting of the American Educational Research Association, New Orleans, LA.

Carnegie Commission on Teaching as a Profession. (1986). *A nation prepared: Teachers for the 21st century.* Hyattsville, MD: Carnegie Forum on Education and the Economy.

Chapman, J. D. (1988). Decentralization, devolution, and the teacher: Participation by teachers in the decision making of schools. *Journal of Educational Administration, 26*(1), 39-72.

Christensen, G. (1992, April). *The changing role of the administrator in an accelerated school.* Paper presented at the annual meeting of the American Educational Research Association, San Francisco.

Chubb, J. E., & Moe, T. M. (1986). No school is an island: Politics, markets, and education. *Brookings Review, 4*(4), 21-28.

Clift, R., Johnson, M., Holland, P., & Veal, M. L. (1992). Developing the potential for collaborative school leadership. *American Educational Research Journal, 29*(4), 877-908.

Conley, D. T., & Goldman, P. (1994). Ten propositions for facilitative leadership. In J. Murphy & K. S. Louis (Eds.), *Reshaping the principalship: Insights from transformational reform efforts* (pp. 237-262). Thousand Oaks, CA: Corwin.

Conley, S. C., & Bacharach, S. (1990). From school-site management to participatory school-site management. *Phi Delta Kappan, 71*(7), 539-554.

Crowson, R. L., & Porter-Gehrie, C. (1980). The discretionary behavior of principals in large-city schools. *Educational Administration Quarterly, 16*(1), 45-69.

Deal, T., & Kennedy, A. (1984). *Corporate cultures: The rites and rituals of corporate life.* Reading, MA: Addison-Wesley.

Duke, D., Showers, B. K., & Imber, M. (1980). Teachers and shared decision making: The costs of involvement. *Educational Administration Quarterly, 16*(1), 93-106.

Dunlap, D. M., & Goldman, P. (1991). Rethinking power in schools. *Educational Administration Quarterly, 27*(1), 5-29.

Edmonds, R. (1979). Effective schools for the urban poor. *Educational Leadership, 37*(1), 15-24.

Education Commission of the States. (1990). *State policy and the school principal.* Denver, CO: Author.

Etheridge, C. P., & Hall, M. L. (1991, April). *The nature, role, and effect of competition, cooperation, and comprehension in multiple site implementation of SBDM.* Paper presented at the annual meeting of the American Educational Research Association, Chicago.

Firestone, W. A., & Wilson, B. L. (1985). Using bureaucratic and cultural linkages to improve instruction: The principal's contribution. *Educational Administration Quarterly, 21*(2), 7-30.

Foa, U., & Foa, E. (1974). *Societal structures of the mind.* Springfield, IL: Charles C Thomas.

Foskett, J. M. (1967). *The normative world of the elementary school principal.* Eugene: University of Oregon, Center for the Advanced Study of Educational Administration.

Foster, W. (1986). *Paradigms and promises: New approaches to educational administration.* Buffalo, NY: Prometheus.

Freeman, D. J., Brimhall, P. A., & Neufeld, J. (1994, April). *Who's in charge now? A principal's endeavors to empower teachers.* Paper presented at the annual meeting of the American Educational Research Association, New Orleans, LA.

Freire, P. (1970). *Pedagogy of the oppressed.* New York: Seabury.

French, J. R., & Raven, B. H. (1959). Bases of social power. In D. Cartwright & A. Zander (Eds.), *Group dynamics: Research and theory* (pp. 259-270). New York: Harper & Row.

Giroux, H. (1992). Educational leadership and the crisis of democratic government. *Educational Researcher, 21*(4), 4-11.

Gitlin, A., Bringhurst, K., Burns, M., Cooley, V., Myers, B., Price, K., Russell, R., & Tiess, P. (1992). *Teachers' voices for school change: An introduction to educative research.* New York: Teachers College Press.

Glaser, B. G. (1978). *Theoretical sensitivity: Advances in the methodology of grounded theory.* Mill Valley, CA: Sociology Press.

Glaser, B. G., & Strauss, A. L. (1967). *The discovery of grounded theory: Strategies for qualitative research.* Chicago: Aldine.

Glickman, C. D. (1993). *Renewing America's schools: A guide for school-based action.* San Francisco: Jossey-Bass.

Glickman, C. D., Allen, L. R., & Lunsford, B. F. (1994). Voices of principals in democratically transformed schools. In J. Murphy & K. S. Louis (Eds.), *Reshaping the principalship: Insights from transformational reform efforts* (pp. 203-218). Thousand Oaks, CA: Corwin.

Goldman, P., Dunlap, D. M., & Conley, D. T. (1991, April). *Administrative facilitation and site-based school reform projects.* Paper presented at the annual meeting of the American Educational Research Association, Chicago.

Goldring, E. B. (1992). System-wide diversity in Israel: Principals as transformational and environmental leaders. *Journal of Educational Administration, 30*(3), 49-62.

Goodlad, J. (1983). *A place called school.* New York: McGraw-Hill.

Goodman, J., Kuzmic, J., & Wu, X. (1992). *Elementary schooling for critical democracy.* New York: State University of New York Press.

Green, J. (Ed.). (1986). *What's next? More leverage for teachers.* Denver, CO: Education Commission of the States.

Greenfield, W. D. (1982, April). *Empirical research on principals: The state of the art.* Paper presented at the annual meeting of the American Educational Research Association, New York.

Gross, N., & Herriott, R. (1965). *Staff leadership in public schools: A sociological inquiry.* New York: John Wiley.

Hall, G. E. (1992). Hank: A 1990's principal. In F. W. Parkay & G. E. Hall (Eds.), *Becoming a principal: The challenges of beginning leadership* (pp. 224-262). Boston: Allyn & Bacon.

Hallinger, P., & Hausman, C. (1993). The changing role of a principal in a school of choice. In J. Murphy & P. Hallinger (Eds.), *Restructuring schooling: Learning from ongoing efforts* (pp. 114-142). Newbury Park, CA: Corwin.

Hallinger, P., & Richardson, D. (1988). Models of shared leadership: Evolving structures and relationships. *Urban Review, 20*(4), 229-245.

Hemphill, J. K., Griffiths, D. E., & Frederiksen, N. (1962). *Administrative performance and personality.* New York: Teachers College Press.

Hess, G. A., & Easton, J. Q. (1991, April). *Who's making what decisions: Monitoring authority shifts in Chicago school reform.* Paper presented at the annual meeting of the American Educational Research Association, Chicago.

Holmes Group Executive Board. (1986). *Tomorrow's teachers: A report of the Holmes Group.* East Lansing, MI: Author.

Homans, G. (1958). Social behavior as exchange. *American Journal of Sociology, 63*(6), 597-606.

Hoy, W. K., & Brown, B. L. (1988). Leadership behavior of principals and the zone of acceptance of elementary teachers. *Journal of Educational Administration, 26*(1), 22-38.

Johnston, G. S., & Venable, B. P. (1986). A study of teacher loyalty to the principal: Rule administration and hierarchical influence of the principal. *Educational Administration Quarterly, 22*(4), 4-27.

Kasten, K. L., Short, P. M., & Jarmin, H. (1989). Self-managing groups and the professional lives of teachers. *Urban Review, 21*(2), 63-80.

Keith, N. Z. (1994). *A critical perspective on teacher participation in urban schools.* Unpublished manuscript.

Kipnis, D. (1976). *The powerholders.* Chicago: University of Chicago Press.

Kirby, P. C., & Colbert, R. (1992, April). *Principals who empower teachers.* Paper presented at the annual meeting of the American Educational Research Association, San Francisco.

Kreisberg, S. (1992). *Transforming power: Domination, empowerment and education.* Albany: State University of New York Press.

Leithwood, K., & Jantzi, D. (1990, April). *Transformational leadership: How principals can help reform school cultures.* Paper presented at the annual meeting of the American Educational Research Association, Boston.

Leithwood, K., Jantzi, D., & Dart, B. (1991, February). *How the school improvement strategies of transformational leaders foster teacher development.* Paper presented at the sixth annual conference of the Department of Educational Administration and Center for Educational Leadership, Ontario Institute for Studies in Education, Toronto, Ontario, Canada.

Lieberman, A. (1988). Teachers and principals: Turf, tension, and new tasks. *Phi Delta Kappan, 69*(9), 648-663.

Lightfoot, S. L. (1983). *The good high school: Portraits of character and culture.* New York: Basic Books.

Lindle, J. C. (1991). *The micropolitics of race and governance in a rural school district: A case study.* Unpublished manuscript, University of Kentucky.

Lindle, J. C. (1992, April). *The effects of shared decision making on instructional leadership: Case studies of the principal.* Paper presented at the annual meeting of the American Educational Research Association, San Francisco.

Lipham, J., & Franks, D. (1966). Nonverbal behavior of administrators. *Educational Administration Quarterly, 2*(2), 101-109.

Lortie, D. C. (1975). *Schoolteacher: A sociological study.* Chicago: University of Chicago Press.

Lukes, S. (1974). *Power: A radical view.* London: Macmillan.

Maeroff, G. I. (1988). *The empowerment of teachers: Overcoming the crisis of confidence.* New York: Teachers College Press.

Malen, B., & Ogawa, R. (1988). Professional-patron influence on site-based governance councils: A confounding case study. *Educational Evaluation and Policy Analysis, 10*(4), 251-270.

Martin, O. L. (1990, April). *Instructional leadership behaviors that empower teacher effectiveness.* Paper presented at the annual meeting of the American Educational Research Association, New Orleans, LA.

Martin, O. L. (1990, November). *Instructional leadership behaviors that empower teacher effectiveness.* Paper presented at the annual meeting of the Mid-South Educational Research Association, New Orleans, LA.

Martin, W. J., & Willower, D. J. (1981). The managerial behavior of high school principals. *Educational Administration Quarterly, 17*(1), 69-90.

McPherson, R. B., & Crowson, R. L. (1994). The principal as mini-superintendent under Chicago school reform. In J. Murphy & K. S. Louis (Eds.), *Reshaping the principalship: Insights from transformational reform efforts* (pp. 57-76). Thousand Oaks, CA: Corwin.

McPherson, R. B., Salley, C., & Baehr, M. E. (1975). What principals do: A national occupational analysis of the school principalship. *Consortium Currents, 2*(1), 1-10.

Mead, G. H. (1934). *Mind, self, and society.* Chicago: University of Chicago Press.

Melenyzer, B. J. (1990, November). *Teacher empowerment: The discourse, meanings and social actions of teachers.* Paper presented at the meeting of the National Council of States on Inservice Education, Orlando, FL.

Metz, M. H. (1978). *Classrooms and corridors: The crisis of authority in desegregated secondary schools.* Berkeley: University of California Press.

Mintzberg, H. (1973). *The nature of managerial work.* New York: Harper & Row.

Morris, V. C., Crowson, R. L., Porter-Gehrie, C., & Hurwitz, E. (1984). *Principals in action: The reality of managing schools.* Columbus, OH: Charles E. Merrill.

Murphy, J., & Louis, K. S. (Eds.). (1994). *Reshaping the principalship: Insights from transformational reform efforts.* Thousand Oaks, CA: Corwin.

Parkay, F. W., & Hall, G. E. (1992). *Becoming a principal: The challenges of beginning leadership.* Boston: Allyn & Bacon.

Peterson, K. D. (1978). The principal's tasks. *Administrator's Notebook, 26*(8), 1-4.

Peterson, K. D., & Warren, V. D. (1994). Changes in school governance and principals' roles: Changing jurisdictions, new power dynamics, and conflict in restructured schools. In J. Murphy & K. S. Louis (Eds.), *Reshaping the principalship: Insights from transformational reform efforts* (pp. 219-236). Thousand Oaks, CA: Corwin.

Prestine, N. A. (1991, October). *Shared decision making in restructuring essential schools: The role of the principal.* Paper presented at the annual conference of the University Council for Educational Administration, Baltimore.

Program for School Improvement. (1993). *Program for school improvement.* Athens: University of Georgia.

Purkey, S., & Smith, M. (1983). Effective schools: A review. *Elementary School Journal, 83,* 427-452.

Reitzug, U. C. (1994). A case study of empowering principal behavior. *American Educational Research Journal, 31*(2), 283-307.

Reitzug, U. C., & Capper, C. A. (1993). *Deconstructing site-based management: Possibilities for emancipation and alternative means of control.* Unpublished manuscript.

Reitzug, U. C., & Cross, B. E. (1994, April). *A multi-site case study of site-based management in urban schools.* Paper presented at the annual meeting of the American Educational Research Association, New Orleans, LA.

Reitzug, U. C., & Reeves, J. E. (1992). "Miss Lincoln Doesn't Teach Here": A descriptive narrative and conceptual analysis of a principal's symbolic leadership behavior. *Educational Administration Quarterly, 28*(2), 185-219.

Rice, E. M., & Schneider, G. T. (1991, April). *A decade of teacher empowerment: An empirical analysis of teacher involvement in decision making.* Paper presented at the annual meeting of the American Educational Research Association, San Francisco.

Roberts, L. (1990, September). Reinventing school leadership. *Proceedings of the Reinventing School Leadership Conference* (pp. 132-136). Cambridge, MA: National Center for Educational Leadership.

Robertson, P. J., & Briggs, K. L. (1993, April). *Managing change through school-based management.* Paper presented at the annual meeting of the American Educational Research Association, New Orleans, LA.

Schlechty, P. C. (1990). *Schools for the twenty-first century: Leadership imperatives for educational reform.* San Francisco: Jossey-Bass.

Schon, D. (1987). *Educating the reflective practitioner.* San Francisco: Jossey-Bass.

Sergiovanni, T. J., & Corbally, J. L. (1984). *Leadership and organizational culture: New perspectives on administrative theory and practice.* Urbana: University of Illinois Press.

Smith, J., & Blase, J. (1991). From empiricism to hermeneutics: Educational leadership as a practical and moral activity. *Journal of Educational Administration, 29*(1), 6-21.

Smylie, M. A., & Crowson, R. L. (1993, April). *Principal assessment under restructured governance.* Paper presented at the annual meeting of the American Educational Research Association, New Orleans, LA.

Sparks, A. C. (1988). The micropolitics of innovation in the physical education curriculum. In J. Evans (Ed.), *Teacher, teaching and control in physical education* (pp. 157-177). Lewes, England: Falmer.

Tesch, R. (1988, April). *The contribution of a qualitative method: Phenomenological research.* Paper presented at the annual meeting of the American Educational Research Association, New Orleans, LA.

Walberg, H. J., & Niemiec, R. P. (1994). Is Chicago school report working? *Phi Delta Kappan, 75*(9), 713-715.

Weick, K. E. (1976). Educational organizations as loosely coupled systems. *Administrative Science Quarterly, 21*(1), 1-18.

Winter, D. G. (1973). *The power motive.* New York: Free Press.

Wohlstetter, P., Smyer, R., & Mohrman, S. A. (1994, April). *New boundaries for school-based management: The high involvement model.* Paper presented at the annual meeting of the American Educational Research Association, New Orleans, LA.

Wolcott, H. F. (1973). *The man in the principal's office: An ethnography.* New York: Holt, Rinehart & Winston.

Index